DALE CARNEGIE'S

BIOGRAPHICAL
ROUNDUP

DALE CARNEGIE'S

BIOGRAPHICAL ROUNDUP

HIGHLIGHTS IN THE LIVES OF FORTY FAMOUS PEOPLE

Essay Index Reprint Series

BOOKS FOR LIBRARIES PRESS
FREEPORT, NEW YORK

INTERNATIONAL STANDARD BOOK NUMBER:

0-8369-1788-X

LIBRARY OF CONGRESS CATALOG CARD NUMBER:

77-117764

PRINTED IN THE UNITED STATES OF AMERICA

CONTENTS

HE WAS TOO SHY TO CALL ON HIS FRIENDS, BUT HE BECAME THE MOST BRILLIANT SPEAKER OF THE AGE

I KNOW OF ONLY TWO MEN who are so famous that they are frequently referred to by their initials only. Who do you suppose they are? One is an American, F. D. R.—Franklin D. Roosevelt. The other is an Irishman. His initials are G. B. S., and he is probably the most famous living literary man in all the world. The story of his incredible career has been told in a book that doesn't even use his name in the title, merely the initials, G. B. S.—George Bernard Shaw.

Shaw's life is full of sharp and striking contrasts. For example, he attended school only five years; yet in spite of his lack of formal education, he made himself one of the most distinguished writers of the age and was awarded the highest honor that can be bestowed upon any author, the Nobel Prize for Literature. The prize carries a cash award of 35,000 dollars, but George Bernard Shaw felt he didn't need either the cash or the honor. So he refused to accept the money. Finally, he was persuaded to accept the 35,000 dollars in cash for a fraction of a second before passing it on to the Anglo-Swedish Literary Alliance.

Bernard Shaw's father came from a fine Irish family, but his mother was disinherited by a rich aunt because she did not approve of the marriage. The family finances got so low that Bernard had to go to work when he was fifteen. For the first year, he worked as a clerk for four dollars and a half a month.

1

Then from his sixteenth to his twentieth year, he took, in an emergency, a responsible man's job as cashier-factotum, and held it down for eight dollars a week. But he hated office work; for he had been reared in a home where candles were burned before the high altar of art and music and literature. When he was seven years old, Bernard Shaw was reading Shakespeare, Bunyan, the Arabian Nights and the Bible. At twelve he was full of Byron. Dickens, Dumas, and Shelley came in his early teens. By the time he was eighteen, he had read Tyndall, Stuart Mill, and Herbert Spencer. The great writers had quickened his imagination and filled him with the stuff that dreams are made of; so during the dreary years when he was slaving for a leading estate agent and private banker, he took no interest in his work; his imagination dwelt entirely in the fairylands of literature and art, science and religion.

Shortly before his twentieth birthday, G. B. S. said to himself: "I have only one life to live.and I am not going to spend it at an office desk."

So in 1876 he burnt his bridges and went to London where his mother was then making her living giving singing lessons. There Bernard Shaw started out on a literary career that was destined to bring him millions of dollars and make his name famous all over the world.

But he wrote for nine years before he could make a living at writing. He devoted all his time to writing, forced himself to write five pages every day regardless of whether he felt like it or not. Just five pages, no more. Shaw said: "I had so much of the schoolboy and clerk still in me that if my five pages ended in the middle of a sentence, I did not finish the sentence until the next day."

He wrote five long novels—one was entitled *Love among the Artists*—and sent the manuscripts to every publisher both in England and in America. They all returned the novels; but the most important of them intimated that they would like to see his next attempt. The oftener he tried them, the more they

2

were set against him; but they did not question his literary competence. His ideas were the difficulty.

Bernard Shaw was so impecunious at the time that he often found it difficult to dig up the postage stamps necessary to mail a manuscript to a publisher. His total income for the first nine years that he devoted to writing was only thirty dollars, or about a penny a day.

When his clothes wore out, he tramped the streets of London with carefully concealed holes in the soles of his shoes and even in the seat of his trousers; but he was never hungry. His mother could always get enough credit from the baker and greengrocer to save him from that extremity.

During those nine years when he was writing novels, he was once paid twenty-five dollars for writing an article on patent medicine, commissioned by a lawyer for heaven knows what purpose. At another time he earned five dollars for counting votes on election day.

How then did Shaw get the money to live? He frankly admits that his family urgently needed his support—needed it desperately; but he did nothing to help support the family. Instead he let the family support him. As Shaw himself says: "I did not throw myself into the struggle for life. I threw my mother into it."

Shaw became self-supporting as a critic of all the fine arts in turn. His first big financial success came not from writing novels but from writing plays. His early plays were all failures. In fact, Shaw wrote for twenty-one years before he made enough to enable him to marry a rich woman without being looked upon as a matrimonial adventurer.

It is almost inconceivable that Bernard Shaw, who has had the brass and audacity to stand before large audiences and denounce the marriage laws, the religious institutions, the democratic shibboleths, and almost all the other cherished traditions of mankind—it is almost incredible that he, of all men, should ever have suffered from shyness and timidity and an inferiority complex. But he did. He suffered intensely from his timidity. For example, as a young man, Bernard Shaw sometimes went to call on friends living on the banks of the Thames River in London. Here is Shaw's own description of how he acted and felt on such occasions.

"I suffered such agonies of shyness that I sometimes walked up and down the Embankment for twenty minutes or more before venturing to knock at the door. Indeed I should have given it up altogether and hurried home asking myself what was the use of torturing myself when it was so easy to run away, if I had not been instinctively aware that I must never let myself off in this manner if I ever meant to do anything in the world. Few men have suffered more than I did in my youth from simple cowardice or have been more horribly ashamed of it."

Yet Bernard Shaw had been so careful about his behavior in society that he studied every book on etiquette that he could find in the world-famous library of the British Museum. The only one that helped him was entitled: *The Manners and Tone of Good Society.*

Finally he hit upon the best and quickest and surest way ever yet devised to conquer timidity and fear. He learned to speak in public. He joined a debating society. The first few times he rose to speak, he produced an impression of such brazen assurance that he was asked to take the chair at the next meeting, yet he was so nervous that he could hardly sign the minutes with his trembling hand. Without notes, he couldn't remember what he intended to say; and with them he could not read them. But still nobody suspected his pitiable condition: he was always listened to. And so fierce was his determination to conquer his shyness and self-consciousness that he attended every meeting in London where there was to be a public discussion and always arose and took part in the debate. Then one evening when Shaw was twenty-six, he heard Henry George, the author of *Progress and Poverty,* preach on his theory of the single tax.

Shaw was started on the track of political economy by this

4

address and at once began preaching land nationalization. When he tried it on the Social-Democrats, they told him that no one was qualified to discuss the single tax question until he had read Karl Marx as well as George's *Progress and Poverty.* Shaw then read a book that has had a profound effect upon history—a book that had a lot to do with the Russian Revolution—a book that shook the world. The book I refer to was written by Karl Marx, and the title of the book is *Capital or a Critique of Political Economy.* Shaw himself has told how the reading of that book affected all his after life. He said: "Reading *Das Kapital* was the turning point in my career. Marx was a revelation. His abstract economics, I discovered later, were wrong; but he rent the veil. He opened my eyes to the facts of history and civilization, gave me an entirely fresh conception of them, and provided me with a purpose and a mission in life. In short, he made a man of me."

Yes, Bernard Shaw was on fire now—on fire with a conviction, a cause. Shy? Timid? No more. That was all gone. Shaw had gotten hold of a book—or, to put it more precisely, a book had gotten hold of Shaw—a book that filled him with the zeal of a crusader and made him forget all about himself. Nothing mattered but the cause; and almost every other night for twelve years, Shaw stood at street corners or in the public halls and even the churches all over England and Scotland preaching socialism, debating with hecklers, tossing off the insults of the unbelievers, and making himself one of the most brilliant speakers and debaters of the age. At last he was in such demand as a speaker that his proletarian audiences were crowded out by plutocratic ones; and he found he was being used as a moneymaker, though he never accepted payment for his talks. He would pass the hat and take up a collection for the cause, but nothing for himself.

In 1896 Shaw met a Miss Charlotte Payne-Townshend. He was a bachelor of forty and she was a maiden lady of thirty-nine. She had inherited a substantial income. Shaw had just made

100,000 dollars in one year by the success of a play in America. She had grown tired of society life and had been swept off her feet by Fabian Socialism. She grew fond of Shaw and told him so. And she also called him a brute and accused him of being the most self-centered man she had ever met.

Two years passed; and Shaw never dreamt of marrying. So in March, 1898, she left for Rome to study its municipal institutions. When she reached Rome, she got a telegram telling her that Shaw was seriously ill. Hurrying back to London, she found him overworked and on the verge of a general breakdown in health. She was shocked at the condition of the tiny room where he worked.

Shaw himself declared that the room could be cleaned by nothing less than a stick of dynamite. He said: "If seven maids with seven mops swept my den for half a century, they would make no impression on it."

When the rich, green-eyed Miss Payne-Townshend insisted on getting him out of that squalor and taking him to her own house in the country where she could nurse him back to health, he sent her out to buy a ring and a wedding license.

Shaw said: "I married her for a reason that I never thought possible: namely, that I had to think more of somebody else than I did of myself."

They lived happily together for forty-five years until the death of Mrs. Shaw on September 12, 1943. Everybody had believed that she was twenty years younger than he, and that he would go first; but actually there was a difference in their ages of but four months.

Although Shaw was born in 1856, he still declares he is too busy to think of death. "I rejoice," he says, "in life for its own sake. Life is no 'brief candle' for me. It is sort of a splendid torch, which I have got hold of for the moment; and I want to make it burn as brightly as possible before handing it on to future generations."

HE SOLD PLANES TO SOUTH AMERICA
THE NORTH AMERICAN WAY

THE DAY THE JAPS struck Pearl Harbor, Jimmy Doolittle was a Major in the Air Corps Reserve. He said to friends: "I'm going to get into this thing with both feet. I'm going to Tokyo with a load of bombs."

Exactly four months and eleven days later he did go to Tokyo with a load of bombs, the first bombs ever to fall upon Japan throughout the 2600 years of its history—bombs that threw Tokyo into a panic—bombs that left a battleship in flames, smashed an airplane factory, and sent the smoke from oil tanks roaring thousands of feet into the air. The raid was so destructive that the officer in charge of the Japanese anti-aircraft defenses committed suicide.

Doolittle was made a brigadier-general and commander of the American Strategic Air Force in North Africa. His bombers protected our troops while they were landing in Sicily and his planes helped bring Italy to her knees.

I had the privilege of interviewing Jimmy Doolittle some years ago. He is one of the most astonishing men I have ever known. The most astonishing incident I know about him occurred years ago down in South America, in Chile. A group of aviators from North America, South America, and Europe were having a party in a hotel. Everybody was showing off, and Jimmy Doolittle, who is something of an acrobat, hopped up on the window sill two stories above the street and stood on his

7

hands. Then he caught hold of each side of the window, straightened his body out slowly, and held himself horizontal over the street below. It was a summer hotel and the wooden frame of the window was old and flimsy; it suddenly broke. Jimmy caught hold of the window sill and hung dangling in the air with nothing but daylight between him and the concrete sidewalk twenty-five feet below. A moment later his fingers gave way and he crashed to the pavement. He broke both of his ankles. In describing the fall, Jimmy said: "As I hit the sidewalk, I met my broken ankles coming up."

If I had found myself dangling in the air twenty-five feet above the sidewalk, I certainly would have yelled for help. I asked Jimmy Doolittle's wife why Jimmy didn't call for help when he knew he was going to fall. She told me that Jimmy would rather have died than have called for help.

That accident happened about twenty years ago, and his wife says that Jimmy's ankles still hurt him after a long walk on the hard pavement.

What was Jimmy Doolittle doing down in Chile? He had been sent there to get orders for American planes in competition with those of European manufacturers. Crack pilots from Germany and England and France were there to demonstrate the superiority of their planes before the President of Chile.

The day set for demonstration arrived. No one imagined that Jimmy Doolittle would be in on the show. How could he? He was in the hospital with two broken ankles. But Jimmy fooled them. He got hold of a hacksaw, sawed the plaster casts off his ankles, had himself carried to the flying field and lifted bodily into the cockpit. Then, with his ankles strapped to the rudder rod, he put on a cat-and-dog fight up in the air such as South America had never seen before. He got his orders all right, and he sold his planes. But when he landed, both his ankles were broken all over again. The surgeon back at the hospital was so disgusted he refused to make new plaster casts.

8

Jimmy Doolittle

Jimmy sent a friend out to buy a pair of women's corsets, took the steel braces out of the corsets, and bound them tightly around his ankles. Then he had himself lifted into his plane once more and, without a word to anyone, flew fifteen hundred miles across the Andes into Bolivia to sell planes to the Bolivian Government. He not only flew to Bolivia, but, when the Bolivians decided that he was a spy and wanted to lynch him, he turned around and flew back to Chile again—all with two broken ankles fastened to the rudder bar with iron clamps!

The first school that Jimmy Doolittle ever attended was in Alaska. He lived in Alaska for eight years because his father had joined the stampede of excited men that poured into Skagway when gold was discovered there.

Jimmy Doolittle, the boy who was destined to grow up and bomb Tokyo, loved the excitement of the rough-and-tumble mining camps of the Far North. He loved to fight, and, since he was the smallest kid attending the school at Nome, he felt he had to demonstrate his superiority by licking the other kids. One Saturday night he licked a couple of boys on a street corner and a policeman threw him in jail. Then he took pity on Jimmy and telephoned his mother.

"Look here, Mrs. Doolittle," the policeman said, "I've got some bad news for you. Your son, Jimmy, is in jail for fighting in the street." This was Saturday night. Jimmy's mother was Irish. She knew her son. "All right, Sergeant," she said, "thanks for calling me up. I'll be down Monday morning in time to get him out for school."

When Jimmy Doolittle returned to California, he won the boxing championship of the high school and decided to take up prize fighting as a career. But his father still had' the excitement of gold in his blood; so he persuaded Jimmy to become a mining engineer. Jimmy studied for three years at the School of Mines in the University of California. Then one afternoon he dropped into the gym where the pick of the middleweights

9

were staging their elimination bouts. The big boxing tournament between Stanford University and the University of California was coming up soon, and California hoped to wipe her ancient rival off the map. The coach cocked his head on one side and sized up Jimmy Doolittle. He was short, but he was all muscle. The coach said: "See here, Doolittle, why don't you box with one of these big fellows? Maybe you can help get him into shape." Jimmy Doolittle waded in and knocked out the first candidate in the first round. Then he tackled the second candidate and knocked him out in the first round. The next day he knocked out the third candidate in the second round.

By that time the University was buzzing with excitement. Jimmy Doolittle, a bantamweight, had staged the fastest series of middleweight elimination bouts that the University of California had ever witnessed.

A few days later the intercollegiate boxing tournament rolled around, and Jimmy Doolittle crawled through the ropes to face his big opponent from Stanford. Jimmy Doolittle was only five feet six and his opponent was almost six feet. The audience laughed. They thought it was a joke. The big fellow from Stanford thought it was a joke, too. What? Was he really expected to fight this little guy? Well, he would play around with him awhile just to amuse the audience.

The gong rang for the start of the fight. Jimmy Doolittle darted in, feinted with his right, planted a crashing left to the big fellow's chin, and sent him down for the count. When the middleweight champion of Stanford University finally regained consciousness, he had lost a complete hour out of his life, the tournament was over, and the audience had gone home to bed.

Brigadier-General James Doolittle has two sons. One is in the Air Corps, and one is in West Point. Jimmy started training them to fight when they were very young. His wife told me that Jimmy used to get down on his knees and teach them to box when they were only six years old.

10

Jimmy Doolittle

Jimmy offered to give his oldest son a pony the day he could knock his dad down. The boy never did win the pony, but, in a friendly bout, he did break one of his dad's teeth. Did Jimmy Doolittle care? Care? He was proud of it! The next day he attended an aviation convention and went around pointing to his broken tooth and bragging, "My kid did that."

Jimmy Doolittle, in his long, tempestuous career, has chalked up five "firsts" in aviation. Here they are:

He was the first man to fly across the American continent in one day.

He was the first to fly the dangerous "outside loop," a stunt so dangerous that aviators believed that it would kill the man who tried it. It didn't kill Jimmy Doolittle, but it did put him in the hospital for a few days.

He was the first to prove that it was practical to fly and to land merely by using instruments, without seeing where you were going.

He was the first to fly a land plane more than 300 miles an hour.

He was the first to bomb Japan.

In spite of all the honors that have been heaped upon him, General Jimmy Doolittle is a very modest man. A few years ago the famous aviator Frank Hawkes was writing a book entitled *Once to Every Pilot.* He insisted on Jimmy Doolittle writing a chapter about his experiences, but Jimmy wrote a chapter about another man's achievements and never even mentioned himself.

Jimmy Doolittle doesn't try to explain away his mistakes or to pass the buck. For example, when Jimmy was a First Lieutenant in the regular Army in 1922, he wrecked a DH-4 plane in a night take-off from Jacksonville, Florida. When his fellow-officers found him standing beside the wrecked plane, they asked what caused the crack-up. Jimmy didn't blame the plane. "Just damn poor piloting, that's all," he replied.

11

Biographical Roundup

When it comes to writing reports, Jimmy Doolittle makes them brief and to the point. During the Cleveland Air Races in 1929, the U. S. Army made a special plane for Doolittle to do stunts in. He never saw the plane until he arrived at the field to put on the show. Hurriedly he took it up for a tryout and came down in a power-dive at three miles a minute. The plane's wing suddenly snapped off; Jimmy was thrown out into space and came down by parachute. He grabbed another plane and put on his show. The Army instructed Jimmy to "report fully" on the accident. Jimmy did. He wrote: "Wings broke, thrown out."

Jimmy likes to play practical jokes. A few years ago he was invited to talk before a convention of dignified scientists and experts in aviation. He talked on the power of modern explosives, exhibited samples, and described the new super-bombs that the Army was producing. Then he held up a little box and said: "But here is a new explosive, the most powerful one ever discovered. If I were to drop this box now, it would blow this hotel to bits." The box actually contained nothing but water. Thirty seconds later a stooge brushed by the speaker's stand and knocked the box to the floor. Jimmy had already arranged to have the house-lights flashed off at that instant, while a friend back-stage fired a double-barreled shotgun loaded with blank cartridges over the heads of the audience. In the excitement one man hit another man's lighted cigar and yelled: "I've been hit!"

Jimmy Doolittle married his high-school sweetheart in 1918, on Christmas Eve. He calls her "the Duchess of Doolittle." I asked the Duchess if Jimmy ever worried and she replied: "I never saw him worry about anything and I never saw him afraid of anything."

The courage of Brigadier-General Jimmy Doolittle is based on knowledge, preparation, and experience.

He was graduated from the Massachusetts Institute of Technology in 1924, with the degree of Master of Science, and the next year was awarded the degree of Doctor of Science by the same school. Three years ago he was elected President of the Institute of Aeronautical Science, one of the highest honors that can be conferred upon any man in the aviation industry.

In the spring of 1942 General Doolittle was awarded another coveted honor, the Guggenheim Medal for "a career distinguished by many outstanding contributions to the aeronautical sciences."

THE WORLD'S MOST FAMOUS WOMAN
SCIENTIST ONCE SLEPT UNDER A
CHAIR TO KEEP WARM

MADAME CURIE, ONE OF THE very few women whose names will probably be remembered for a thousand years, was a shy, timid Polish girl who discovered what the great scientists thought was impossible. She discovered a new element vastly different from any other element known to science—an element that radiated energy incessantly. She named it radium.

Radium's greatest contribution is in the war we are waging against cancer. Countless thousands of cancer patients have either been permanently cured by radium or have had their terrible suffering alleviated, and in many cases their lives lengthened by many years.

While the future Madame Curie was studying physics and mathematics in the University of Paris, she was so poor that she actually fainted from hunger. Wouldn't she have been astonished then if she could have known that fifty-two years later a motion picture company would spend over a million dollars making a picture of her life! Wouldn't she have been astonished if she could have foreseen that she was to become the only person who has twice been given the Nobel Prize for achievement in science! The first time was in 1903 for her outstanding achievement in physics, and the second time in 1911 for her outstanding achievement in chemistry.

Yet Madame Curie probably would never have become a

14

scientist at all nor ever have discovered radium if she had not been insulted, as a young girl, by an arrogant and wealthy family in her native Poland.

The story goes like this:

When the future Madame Curie was a young girl of nineteen, she was employed by a wealthy family in Poland to look after their ten-year-old daughter, to care for her and help her in her studies. When the eldest son of this rich family came home from college for the Christmas holidays, he danced and skated with the new governess; he was charmed by her beautiful manners and delighted with her sparkling wit and poetry. He fell in love with her and proposed marriage, but when his mother heard the news she almost fainted; his father stormed and raged.

What! His son proposing to marry a girl without a penny! A girl without social standing, a girl employed in other people's homes!

The future Madame Curie was stunned by this disgraceful slap in the face—so stunned that she resolved to abandon all thoughts of marriage and to go to Paris to study and devote her life to science.

In 1891 this young Polish woman—Manya Sklodowska she was then—registered for the science course at the University of Paris. She was too shy and timid to make friends, and she was so terribly in earnest she had no time for friends. Every moment she could not consecrate to her studies, she considered lost. For the next four years she had to live on the little money she had saved as a governess, plus the few rubles that her father, a teacher of mathematics in Poland, could send her now and then. She had to live on sixty cents a day—pay for her room, her food, clothes, heat, and expenses at the university. Her room had only one window and that was a skylight. It had no gas, no electric light, and, what was a thousand times worse, it had no heat. She could afford to buy only two sacks of coal throughout the entire winter.

To save her little treasure of coal, she often did not light the stove on winter nights, working her mathematical problems with fingers that were numb and shoulders that were shaking. Then before she went to bed, the future Madame Curie would open her trunk and take out her towels, pillow cases, a sheet, her extra dress, and pile all these things on top of her bed in order to keep warm. But still she shivered. Occasionally she reached for her chair and pulled it on top of the bed, hoping desperately that somehow even a chair would add a bit of warmth to her shaking body.

Not only did she have little food to cook, but she felt it was stealing precious time away from her studies to cook even the little that she had. For weeks at a time she forced her body to get along on nothing but a little bread and butter and weak tea. Often she grew dizzy, stumbled to her bed, and lost consciousness. When she came to her senses, she would ask herself: "Why did I faint?" She was unwilling to admit that her disease was slow starvation. Once she fainted in a class at the University, and when she regained consciousness, she admitted to the doctor that she had lived for days on a few cherries and a bunch of radishes.

But let's not feel too sorry for this student in her Paris garret—this student who was destined ten years later to become the most famous woman in the world. She was so absorbed in her work, so obsessed by a desire for knowledge, that hunger could not make her falter, nor cold dampen the fires that burned within.

Three years after she arrived in Paris, Manya Sklodowska married the only kind of man with whom she could ever have been happy—a man who, like herself, was completely devoted to science. His name was Pierre Curie. He was only thirty-five years old, yet he was one of the most distinguished scientists in France.

The day they were married their total earthly possessions consisted of a couple of bicycles, and they spent their honeymoon

16

bicycling through the French countryside, lunching on bread and cheese and fruit, and spending their nights in village inns where the soft candlelight threw weird shadows on the faded wallpaper.

Three years later, Madame Curie was preparing for her doctor's degree; in order to get the degree of Doctor of Philosophy, she had to do some original scientific research and write a report on it. She decided to devote her research to trying to solve a recently discovered mystery—the mystery of why a metal called uranium gave off rays of light.

It was the beginning of a great scientific adventure, a voyage into the fascinating mysteries of chemistry.

Madame Curie tested all known chemical bodies and she also tested hundreds of minerals to discover if they gave off those mysterious rays; she finally concluded that these powerful rays were shot into space by some unknown element.

Finally, Madame Curie's husband, Pierre Curie, dropped his own experiments to help her search for this mysterious new element.

After months of experiment, Madame Curie and her husband tossed a bombshell into the scientific world. They announced that they believed they had discovered a metal whose radiation was two million times stronger than the radiation of uranium; a metal whose rays could penetrate wood, stone, steel, copper; a miracle metal whose rays could be stopped by nothing except thick sheets of lead. If they had indeed made such a discovery, it would upset all the fundamental theories in which scientists had believed for centuries.

They named their miraculous substance radium.

Nothing remotely like it had ever been known before. It was so sensationally different from all other metals that sober scientists doubted that such a metal could even exist. They demanded proof. Show us pure radium, they said, so we can see it and test it and discover its atomic weight.

So Madame Curie and her husband worked for the next four

years (1898 to 1902) to prove the existence of radium—worked for four years to produce a decigram of radium, a quantity no bigger than half the size of a small pea.

How did they produce it? By boiling down and refining eight tons of ore. They worked in an old abandoned shed that had formerly been used by medical students as a dissecting room; it had been deemed no longer fit for even that work. It had no floor, a leaky roof, an old and totally inadequate stove; in the winter time it was as cold as all outdoors. The bitter smoke from the boiling ores and chemicals stung Madame Curie's eyes and choked her throat. For four years she and her husband worked in that miserable shed. He finally grew discouraged and wanted to give up the search until some more favorable time, but Madame Curie refused to quit; so they persisted until they had actually produced a decigram of radium.

As a result of that discovery, Madame Curie became the most famous and the most distinguished woman on earth. But were those days of glory and honor her happiest? Ah, no; she declared that the happiest years of her life had been the poverty-stricken years when she was working in that miserable old shed with a dirt floor—years when her body often shivered with cold and collapsed with fatigue, but years entirely consecrated to work she loved.

In 1902 Madame Curie and her husband had to decide whether they wanted to be rich, or true to the selfless ideals of scientific research. By that time it had already been discovered that radium was invaluable in treating cancer. There was a growing demand for radium and no one else in the world knew how to produce it except Madame Curie and her husband. They could have patented the technique they had invented for extracting it and have obtained a royalty on every bit of radium produced throughout the world.

Since radium was going to be produced for a profit, few people would have blamed Madame Curie and her husband for

accepting a royalty from the commercial manufacturers. Such
a royalty would have meant economic security for them and
their children, the elimination of drudgery, and the building
of a fine laboratory for further research. But it renews and
deepens one's faith in human nature to know that Madame
Curie refused to accept one penny for her discovery. "It would
be impossible," she said. "It would be contrary to the scientific
spirit. Besides, radium is going to be used in treating disease,
and it would be impossible to take advantage of that."

So, with Christlike unselfishness, she chose forever between
riches and comparative poverty—between a life of ease and a
life of service.

HE MAKES NEWS, BUT HE DOESN'T
LISTEN TO IT

THE NUMBER ONE MILITARY MAN of the United States Army, the man who runs the whole shebang, is General George C. Marshall, Chief of Staff.

What kind of a person is this Number One man of the United States Army? Well, General J. Franklin Bell, who was himself formerly Chief of Staff of the United States Army, worked with General Marshall in the Philippines, and he declared that George Marshall is the greatest military genius that this nation has produced since the days of Stonewall Jackson.

To be compared to Stonewall Jackson as a military leader is high praise indeed. During the Civil War, Stonewall Jackson was the military idol of the South. Abraham Lincoln got down on his knees and asked Almighty God to send him a military genius like Stonewall Jackson to lead the armies of the North. Stonewall Jackson's campaign in the Shenandoah Valley of Virginia is still being studied in the military colleges of Europe as one of the brilliant campaigns of all time.

General Pershing, who led our forces in Europe during the first World War, declared that General Marshall was the best officer in the American Army in 1918. Pershing made Marshall Chief of Operations for the First American Army in Europe; and, in that capacity, he solved brilliantly one of the toughest operating problems of the first World War. Here was the problem:

General George C. Marshall

General Pershing wanted to move more than half a million men, three thousand guns, forty thousand tons of ammunition, and thirty-four hospitals, from St. Mihiel to the Argonne. The problem was to move them so secretly that no enemy spy or enemy aviator would discover the movements. General Marshall did precisely that. In two weeks he moved the troops cross-country secretly by night. The Germans never knew what was happening until half a million American soldiers tore into them on the Meuse-Argonne front in an attack that helped win the war. As Abraham Lincoln said, "How much in military matters depends on one master mind!"

General Marshall believes in discipline, but he doesn't believe in the brutal, insulting manner that some army officers have used since the beginning of time.

When General Marshall became Chief of Staff, he did something that had never been done before in the history of our fighting forces. He sent out a list of 118 questions to three thousand soldiers. He asked the soldiers to answer these questions frankly and not to sign their names. He asked such questions as:

"Do you like your officers?"

"If so, why?"

"If not, why not?"

"How can we make you better soldiers?"

"How can we make the Army a better army?"

This procedure was so unusual that it made some of the old-timers gasp with amazement and snort with disgust. But the results were superb. Army training has been made more human, and men have been encouraged to show more initiative. The results of this training were reflected in all the theaters of war.

I have never had the pleasure of talking to General Marshall personally, but I have had the privilege of talking with his wife. She told me that General Marshall had apparently been born with a desire to be a soldier; that even as a boy in knee pants, he was always playing soldier, always drilling the other boys in

21

the neighborhood to march and to make cavalry charges on their stick horses.

He longed to go to West Point; but in order to enter West Point, he would have to be appointed; and he couldn't get appointed because his father was a southern Democrat in a Republican stronghold in Pennsylvania. So he enrolled in the Virginia Military Institute at Lexington, Virginia, and made himself one of the most popular and respected men in college.

He showed his good sportsmanship by refusing to give the name of a student who had almost killed him in a hazing prank. This student, without meaning to do so, had seriously wounded him with a bayonet. But the future Chief of Staff of the United States Army refused to tell who had done it. His fellow-students tossed their hats into the air. Hurrah for Marshall! A good sport! He could take it on the chin!

George Marshall won the enthusiastic respect of the boys at the Virginia Military Institute by his astonishing achievements in football. During the first three years at college, George Marshall felt he had no time for football. In his senior year, however, he studied the strategy of football for a few weeks and played tackle on the varsity team. Then, in spite of the fact that he weighed only 165 pounds, he outplayed every opponent all season and brought honor and glory to the school by making the All-Southern Team; and for a man who had never handled a football before, that was almost a miracle. I doubt whether any other man ever made a similar record in the history of football.

General Marshall's record at Virginia Military Institute and his flair for leadership won him the position of First Captain, the highest student office and the highest military honor in the Institute.

As Chief of Staff of the largest army in America's history, General George C. Marshall has had to perform a tremendous amount of work each day—carry vast responsibilities that would

General George C. Marshall

have crushed the average man. Yet General Marshall never seems rushed or worried. I asked his wife how he was able to do it. She gave me seven reasons that explain his ability to do an incredible amount of work without nervous or physical exhaustion:

First, he never reads long-winded reports; he reads only reports that are condensed and summarized.

Second, he has trained himself to read rapidly, to concentrate completely, and to make decisions quickly. In fact he does everything rapidly. When he comes home from the office and is going out at night, he will lie down and read and then get up and change his shoes, shirt, and uniform in four minutes flat.

Third, after making a military decision, he never squanders time and energy by reviewing it. Once he has made a decision, he devotes all his time and energy to carrying it out.

Fourth, he has vast and detailed knowledge of military problems. You'll never find any colored pins stuck in the maps on the walls of his office; General Marshall knows from memory where every division is and precisely what it is supposed to do.

Fifth, he believes in starting his long day early. He has breakfast at seven and is at his office by seven-thirty. He once said: "Nobody ever had an original thought after three o'clock in the afternoon."

Sixth, he refreshes himself in the middle of the day by taking a nap. Like Winston Churchill, he rests and relaxes before he gets tired. He walks home to lunch, often taking a top-ranking general home with him; and, as they walk, they may discuss problems of military strategy. Immediately after lunch, General Marshall retires to a sun porch on the second floor of his home, stretches out on a couch, falls asleep, and awakens fifteen minutes later completely refreshed.

And seventh, General Marshall works efficiently because he never worries. Mrs. Marshall said to me: "I have been married to the General for thirteen years, and I have seen him deeply concerned about his problems, but I never saw him lose one second of sleep by worry."

When I asked Mrs. Marshall how her distinguished husband manages to avoid worry, she told me that at the end of the day he cuts himself off from all contact with his office and with his fellow-officers, and he never brings any work home with him at night.

She said that, as a result of years of army discipline, General Marshall has learned to control himself. He knows that worrying would unfit him for his work; so he just doesn't permit himself to worry. Here is an illustration of his self-discipline: He used to smoke two or three packages of cigarettes every day, but seven years ago he decided that smoking was interfering with his efficiency. He forced himself to stop smoking instantly. From that day to this he hasn't smoked at all. Before a general can take a city, he must learn to control himself. General Marshall can do both.

He also keeps from worrying by filling his spare time with interesting activities, such as canoeing, riding horseback, going to the movies, or taking long walks with his wife. He reads in bed for three hours practically every night, always to the accompaniment of soft radio music.

General Marshall's chauffeur frequently goes to the public library and brings home twenty books that the librarian has selected for the General—histories, biographies, and books on current events. The General has a table on each side of his bed, both of them piled high with books. He reads with astonishing speed, devouring a book of two hundred pages in three hours.

The General reads every night until he falls asleep; and, if he awakens during the night, he doesn't worry about insomnia. No, he just turns on the light and reads again until he gets sleepy.

Mrs. Marshall told me that the two men in history who had

influenced General Marshall most were Benjamin Franklin and Robert E. Lee. He has made a special study of Lee's military strategy and he admires Lee's character intensely. Another book that he reads and rereads is Benjamin Franklin's *Autobiography,* one of the classics of American literature.

Mrs. Marshall asked her husband one day what he would prefer to be if he couldn't be a military leader, and he replied, "I would like to be the conductor of a great symphony orchestra."

Such is the story of General George C. Marshall, Chief of Staff of the United States Army—a soldier, as Shakespeare would say, "fit to stand by Caesar and give direction."

HE REFUSED TO INVEST MONEY IN A NEWFANGLED CONTRAPTION CALLED THE TELEPHONE

HOLLYWOOD SPENT TWO MILLION dollars making a film telling the life story of one of the most remarkable men this nation ever produced. He was the most famous literary figure of his generation, and became the most widely read humorous writer of all time.

He attended a log cabin school until he was twelve years old. That was all the formal education he ever had; yet Oxford and Yale Universities gave him honorary degrees, and his companionship was sought by the most learned men on earth. He made millions and millions of dollars by writing books. In fact, the products of his pen have probably made more money than those of any other writer who ever lived. Although he died thirty-four years ago, book royalties and motion picture and radio rights are still pouring a golden flood of dollars into the exchequer of his estate.

This author's real name was Samuel Langhorne Clemens, but he is known to the world as Mark Twain.

Mark Twain's entire life was an adventure. He lived through one of the most picturesque and colorful periods of American history. He was born 110 years ago in a sleepy little Missouri village not far from the Mississippi River—just seven years after the first railway had been built in America; while Abe Lincoln was yet a barefoot farm laborer, walking behind a wooden plow and a team of oxen.

26

Mark Twain

Mark Twain lived seventy-five thrilling years and died in Connecticut in 1910. He wrote twenty-three books. Some of them are already forgotten, but two of his books—*Huckleberry Finn* and *Tom Sawyer*—will probably achieve literary immortality and be read and treasured throughout the centuries, as long as boys are boys. These two books were written out of his own experiences. They weren't exactly written—they exploded from him.

Mark Twain was born in a tiny two-room cabin in Florida, Missouri. Today an up-to-date farmer wouldn't keep even his cows or chickens in the sort of hovel in which Mark Twain lived as a child. Eight people lived in those two dark rooms—the family of seven and a slave girl. Mark Twain was a delicate baby, so sickly that he was not expected to pull through the first winter. As he grew older, Mark Twain became quite a problem. His mother said that he gave her more trouble than all the rest of the family put together. He was always playing practical jokes. He was so bored with school that he sometimes ran away from home, and he always ran toward Old Man River. He was charmed by the mighty Mississippi, with its mysterious islands, its slow-moving rafts, its stately current swinging to the sea. He would sit beside the river for hours and dream. He was nearly drowned nine different times. But while playing Indian and pirates, exploring caves, eating turtle eggs, and drifting down the river on a raft, he was getting the priceless experiences for the scenes and characters that he was to immortalize later in his two most famous books.

Mark Twain inherited his genius for humor from his mother. He once declared that he never saw his father smile; but in speaking of his mother, he said: "She had a sort of ability which is rare in man and almost never found in woman—the ability to say a humorous thing with the perfect air of not knowing it to be humorous." That ability, inherited from her, made Mark Twain one of the most humorous public speakers who ever lived. It enabled him to make a fortune on the public platform. His mother, by the way, was so tender-hearted that she literally refused to kill flies, and even punished the cats for killing mice. She once had to drown some unwanted kittens; but she warmed the water so they would die comfortably.

Mark Twain always despised school. It deprived him of his liberty; it kept him cooped up inside four walls of a log cabin when his heart's desire was to roam the woods and explore the banks of the mysterious Mississippi.

When he was twelve, his chance to escape from the hated confinement of school came as a result of the death of his father.

Realizing that his father was gone for the long forever, he was filled with remorse for his wild days, his disobediences, his unwillingness to do as his father had wished. The sensitive boy wept now with repentance and self-accusation.

His mother, trying to comfort him, said, "What's done is done and it can't matter to your father any longer. Now I want you to promise me . . ."

"I will promise you anything," the boy sobbed, "if you only won't make me go back to school. Anything."

A few days later Mark Twain was apprenticed to a printer with whom his family felt he would make a living and get an education. His pay for the two years of his apprenticeship was to be board and clothes.

Two years after he became a printer, Mark Twain was walking down the streets of Hannibal, Missouri, one afternoon when he picked up a piece of paper that was blowing along the sidewalk—a page that had been torn from a book.

That little incident, trivial as it was, probably affected Mark Twain's career more than any other single act of his life, for that stray bit of paper was a page torn from a biography of Joan of Arc. It told of her being held captive in the fortress at Rouen. The injustice of it all stirred this young boy of fourteen. Who was Joan of Arc? He didn't know. He had never

28

even heard of her. But from then on, he devoured everything that had ever been written about her. His interest in her life story glowed and burned for more than half a lifetime; forty-six years later he wrote a book about her entitled *Recollections of Joan of Arc*. The critics felt that this book was far from his best, but he considered it his masterpiece. He knew that if it were published under his name, people would regard it as a humorous book; and he was so eager to have it taken seriously that he didn't even sign his name to it.

Albert Bigelow Paine says in his four-volume biography of Mark Twain that finding the page about Joan of Arc awakened Mark Twain's interest in all history and fired him with a passion that became "the largest feature of his intellectual life and remained with him until his very last day on earth. From the moment when that fluttering leaf was blown into his hands, his career as one of the mentally elect was assured."

Mark Twain had no more business ability than a Kansas jack-rabbit; he was a sucker for the most fantastic financial schemes. For example: as a result of reading a book, he once got the idea that he could make a fortune collecting and selling cocoa in the steaming jungles along the upper reaches of the Amazon River. He knew nothing about cocoa, had no money to pay for the long trip to South America, and even if he had reached the headwaters of the Amazon, he couldn't have talked to the natives and would probably have died of tropical fever. But incredible as it sounds, he found a fifty-dollar bill blowing down the street one day. He took that fifty dollars and started for the Amazon River. He got as far as Cincinnati and then had to give up the trip because he ran out of money.

Later in life he made vast profits from his books and lectures, but every time he tried to invest his money—well, let me give you some concrete examples. He invested in a patent steam generator that wouldn't generate. He invested in a watch company that didn't tick long enough to pay its first dividend. He invested in a steam pully that wouldn't work. He started a publishing company that failed with a loss of 160,000 dollars. He invested heavily in a machine that was supposed to set type. The only thing it ever set was Mark Twain; it set him back about a fifth of a million dollars.

Then one day Mark Twain met a young inventor named Alexander Graham Bell. Bell tried to persuade Mark Twain to invest his money in a new-fangled invention called the telephone. This man Bell actually claimed that with his invention you could sit in your own house and talk to somebody five blocks away—over a wire. Mark Twain laughed. He might be a fool, but he wasn't an idiot. The very idea of talking five blocks over a wire. Absurd!

If Mark Twain had bought five hundred dollars' worth of telephone stock then, it would be worth untold millions today. Instead of investing the five hundred dollars in telephone stock, however, Mark Twain loaned it to a friend who went bankrupt three days later.

In 1893, when Mark Twain was fifty-eight years old, he found himself overwhelmed with debts. The nation was trembling under the influence of a financial depression and Mark Twain himself was suffering from ill health. He could have by-passed his debts through bankruptcy. But he didn't. Instead, he resolved that he would pay back every cent he owed. How? By writing and by making a lecture tour of the world. Despite his ill health and his hatred of lecturing, he spent five years on a speaking tour, in order to pay his creditors. The tour was a tremendous success. It was almost impossible to find halls large enough to house the crowds that flocked to hear him. When the last dollar was paid, Mark Twain wrote: "I have abundant peace of mind again—no sense of burden. Work has become a pleasure —it is not labor any longer."

Mark Twain was infinitely more fortunate in love, however, than in business. Before he ever saw the girl he married, he fell

Mark Twain

in love with her picture. It happened while he was making a
boat trip to the Holy Land—the trip that resulted in his writing
Innocents Abroad.

One fateful day Mark Twain visited the cabin of his young
friend Charles Langdon and saw there a picture of Langdon's
sister, the beautiful Olivia Langdon. In a flash he knew that
that was the girl he wanted to marry. Again and again, as the
boat trip progressed, he returned to young Langdon's cabin to
look reverently at the miniature, and each time his conviction
deepened that this was the girl for him.

A few months later Mark Twain met Olivia Langdon at a
dinner in New York. Toward the end of his life, he wrote:
"From the day I met her to now, she has never been out of my
mind." Mark Twain was soon invited to visit at her father's
house in Elmira, New York.

When the time came for the end of his visit, he did not want
to leave. He got the Langdon's coachman to fix the carriage seat
so it would upset and dump him out on the ground. Then he
packed his bag, shook hands, climbed into the spring wagon
and waved good-by. The coachman cracked his whip and the
horses lunged forward. The back seat upset and quick as a flash
there was Mark Twain on the ground with his eyes closed, apparently half dead. Well, of course, great excitement ensued.
The family picked him up, carried him inside the house, and
put him to bed. And for two mortal weeks he remained in bed.
There wasn't a thing the matter with him——he'd learned that
carriage trick when he was a boy in Hannibal, Missouri—but he
lay there in bed and let himself be nursed and waited on and
petted by his sweetheart. She called him "Youth, dear" and he
called her "Livy, darling"; and until the time of her death,
thirty-four years later, they were always "Livy, darling" and
"Youth, dear." She kept his love letters locked up in a box;
and every year when they went on their vacation, she sent them
to the bank for safekeeping.

His wife edited all of Mark Twain's manuscripts. At night he took his day's writing and placed it on a stand by the head of her bed so she could read it before she went to sleep. She took out all the cuss words and saw that everything was perfectly proper. No matter what changes she made in his work, he always accepted them without argument.

He had such a horror of losing his manuscripts or misplacing them that he wouldn't let the maid dust his desk. He used to draw a chalk line on the floor, and the maid was forbidden to step across that line.

When Mark Twain reached seventy, he decided that he was old enough to do as he pleased; he ordered fourteen white suits and a hundred white ties, and for the rest of his life he wore nothing but white from head to foot. He even had a white dress suit.

Halley's comet was visible in the sky the night that Mark Twain was born in 1835. It returns every seventy-six years and it was his ambition to live until it appeared again. He did. Halley's comet was glowing in the sky again the night he died in 1910. His last request was that his daughter sing to him the old Scotch airs that he loved so well.

Here are four lines which Mark Twain had engraved on the tombstone of his daughter Susy—lines which a loving nation might well have engraved on his own headstone:

> Warm summer sun, shine kindly here;
> Warm southern wind, blow softly here:
> Green sod above, lie light, lie light!—
> Good night, dear heart, good night, good night.

THEY CALLED IT A SUICIDE BRIGADE—BUT HE BROUGHT 'EM BACK ALIVE!

ONE OF THE MOST COLORFUL and spectacular leaders ever to fight in the jungles of Asia was Major-General Orde Charles Wingate. In 1943, when Wingate was only thirty-nine years old, he led several thousand British jungle fighters across the borders of India and penetrated the Jap lines in Burma. Then, for three months, Wingate and his jungle Commandos cut the Jap lines of supply, exploded their ammunition dumps, wrecked their airfields, dynamited bridges and railways, and raised cain in general. The Japs were stunned, thrown into confusion. They ran like—well, did you ever kick an anthill and then watch the ants running about in bewildered alarm? That's the way the Japs ran when Wingate's Raiders began to strike in the most unexpected places. The Japs outnumbered the Raiders ten to one and could easily have wiped them out if they could have found them. But Wingate's men broke up into various units and scattered, so that finding them was like looking for a needle in ten thousand square miles of dense jungle.

General Wingate and his Raiders accomplished four extremely important things:

First: They kept the Japs so busy trying to preserve their lines of communication in Burma that they had little time to attack the Chinese or to invade India.

Second: They brought back vital information from their raids in Burma that made it possible for the RAF to make effective bombing raids on Jap-held territory.

33

Third: They proved that, with adequate training, even second-line troops such as Wingate had—married men twenty-eight to thirty-five years old who had spent their lives in the shops and factories of England—could lick both the jungle and the Japs.

Fourth: They planned, tested, and perfected the methods which were later used to drive the Japs out of the jungles of Burma.

Yet when General Wingate first proposed his revolutionary ideas for waging war in the jungle, without any lines of communication or supply except by air, some of the more conservative military leaders declared it sounded more like a plot for a Hollywood movie than real war. Some declared that it would be suicidal. Wingate merely took that as challenge, and proceeded to set a new and victorious pattern in modern warfare.

Starting in the summer of 1942, Wingate trained his men in the devastating heat of India for six months. He told them they would have to learn to imitate Tarzan; and they did.

In February, 1943, they penetrated the virgin jungles of Burma, using a combination of the oldest and newest means of transportation that man has ever employed. They used the same kind of pack animals that Alexander the Great used: elephants, mules, and oxen; and they used airplanes to drop supplies from the sky.

Wingate's shock troops pushed through dense jungles, over jagged saw-tooth mountains, and along narrow trails where one false step meant plunging over a precipice. One elephant and one mule did, in fact, lose their footing and hurtle to their deaths far below. They occasionally passed human skeletons— the remains of some of General Stilwell's men who had retreated over these trails the previous summer.

The elephants carried mortars, guns, folding boats, and radio sets. The oxen pulled carts filled with machine guns, ammunition, and dynamite. There were eight columns—columns of

Major-General Wingate

Gurka and Burmese soldiers, English Tommies, elephants, dogs, mules, oxen. Each column was a mile long and looked like a procession headed for Noah's Ark. Yet its movements could not be heard even two hundred yards away, for the thick, soft jungle deadens all sound.

Wingate's Raiders frequently marched thirty miles a day in a devastating heat that sent the thermometer above 105. Wingate had the strange theory that sickness could be prevented by constant marching. He wouldn't permit his men to shave because shaving meant ten minutes less marching or sleeping.

Scouting dogs were sent ahead of each column. These dogs were trained to detect the scent of a Jap just as other dogs are trained to recognize the scent of a fox or a pheasant.

Each man carried on his back enough food to last six days. After that, they had to depend on supplies dropped from the clouds. A radio operator sent code messages indicating the exact spots where supplies were to be dropped—places such as dried-up river beds, rice fields, and fields of waving elephant grass. Smoke fires indicated the exact spots for day delivery and flares were used at night. Over half a million pounds of supplies were dropped by airplane.

No matter what the boys requested, headquarters in India did all in its power to deliver the goods. Planes delivered such items as false teeth, a monocle, and a biography of Bernard Shaw. One officer, whose forces were surrounded by the Japs, radioed a request for a last will that he wanted to sign; it was sent. So were four hundred pounds of chocolates that the men requested, although a restaurant in Calcutta had to work all night to make the chocolates.

The officer in charge of supplies in India was a Captain Lord. One day Wingate radioed a message saying: "Oh Lord, send us bread." Back came the answer: "The Lord hath heard thy prayer." A few hours later the bread was dropped out of the sky—manna from heaven.

35

Biographical Roundup

After marching through three hundred miles of enemy-held territory, killing a thousand Japs, cutting supply lines, and destroying vital military installations, Wingate's Raiders were finally ordered to return home. There is an old military proverb that says: "Assemble to fight but scatter to live." After their objectives were accomplished, therefore, Wingate's men scattered and broke up into parties of forty men each. They knew that if they traveled with oxen and mules loaded down with radios and heavy equipment, they could travel only a third as fast as by traveling without animals and heavy supplies. Speed was vital, so they buried their radios, smashed their heavy equipment, killed and ate their mules and oxen, and then started the long, terrible hike back to India. Since they had no radios, they couldn't possibly get any supplies. They became so hungry that they had to eat snakes, vultures, roots dug up in the jungles, and soup made from grass. Each man lost an average of fifteen pounds in weight. Their stomachs shrank to one-half normal size. Since the Japs were waiting for them around every water hole, they had to march for days in the terrible heat with only a few mouthfuls of water that they found in hollow bamboos.

When Wingate and his men reached India in May, 1943, they were greeted with loud acclaim. Wingate was called "The Lawrence of Burma," after the famous "Lawrence of Arabia" of the first World War. The grateful people of Burma called him "The Lord Protector of the Pagodas."

Wingate was born in India, six thousand feet above sea-level, high in the Himalayas. His father, after serving in the British Army for thirty-two years, retired and founded a religious mission in India. Wingate was brought up in puritanical ways. Even during his toughest campaigns, he started each day with prayer and took passages from the Bible to make up the code he used in his radio messages. He was a fanatic about physical health. He used to massage his body with a wire brush, even when talking to newspaper reporters. He refused to smoke, but he had a firm conviction that onions bucked you up, so he used to have a few onions flown out with the rest of the supplies, and he ate the onions as he marched.

He was a great reader. He had an extraordinary memory and knew by heart the army manuals of all the great powers and the lives of great generals all the way back to the Pharaohs of Egypt. His literary tastes ranged from Shakespeare, philosophy, and religious history to comic strips. He often talked like an encyclopedia, holding forth in the officers' mess on everything from hyenas to Hamlet. He could speak several languages and could even sing in Arabic.·

While preparing for one of his guerilla campaigns, he carried an alarm clock around in his hand all day to remind everyone that precious minutes were ticking by.

He violated a sacred rule of British military conduct by telling his superiors right to their faces of their military blunders; they considered him an upstart and a madman. He is probably the only British officer of modern times who used his ancient prerogative of writing to the King himself about the mistakes of a superior officer. As it happened, one of the men on the committee which had to advise the King about how to treat Wingate's letter, was the very man he had criticized. He would probably have had Wingate dismissed from the army had it not been for his outstanding military ability. Wingate once remarked solemnly to a friend: "I am not half so crazy as people think."

Winston Churchill certainly didn't think he was crazy. After Wingate returned from the Burmese jungles, Churchill ordered him flown to the first Quebec Conference. There, Churchill, Wingate, and other military leaders planned the next vital campaign against the Japs in northern Burma, a campaign fought by glider troops dropped into the jungles by air and supplied by air.

Major-General Orde Charles Wingate was killed in an airplane crash near the border of India on March 24, 1944. But his soul goes marching on in the men he trained and in the spirit and inspiration and tradition he left behind. He called his men Chindits, after the terrible stone dragons that guard the sacred temples of Burma. What a pity that General Wingate didn't live to see the magnificent show his Chindits put on after his death!

Wingate will probably go down in British military history along with such legendary personalities as Clive of India, Wolfe of Quebec, Chinese Gordon, and Lawrence of Arabia. His life was a living example of his favorite quotation: "Whatsoever thy hand findeth to do, do it with all thy might."

HE ONCE RODE A MULE TO A COUNTRY SCHOOL—YET HE EARNED HALF A MILLION DOLLARS IN FOUR MINUTES

I ONCE HAD DINNER with a man who upon one occasion was paid more than two thousand dollars a second for his work— more than two thousand dollars a second for 237 seconds, or a total of half a million dollars for less than four minutes' work. His name is Jack Dempsey. Jack Dempsey is more than a man. He is an American tradition.

I had dinner with him at the training headquarters of the United States Coast Guard at Manhattan Beach in Brooklyn, where he was a lieutenant commander in the United States Coast Guard and was training thousands of men in the art of boxing and wrestling and jujitsu.

In the early days of the war, Jack Dempsey's popularity was demonstrated when a newspaper story telling about his work with the Coast Guard appeared in the Middle West. The story appeared on Saturday after the local recruiting station had closed for the day, and caused such a stir that early the next morning—Sunday morning—the editor was called at his home and told that more than 250 men and boys were storming the closed recruiting station. The editor phoned the authorities and the station was opened to receive the enlistments of these men and boys wanting to get in the Coast Guard, where they could be trained under the direction of Jack Dempsey.

39

Biographical Roundup

Jack Dempsey told me that the most trying and discouraging years of his life came immediately after he had defeated Jess Willard and had become heavyweight champion of the world.

He discovered then what many other people have discovered: that there is often more pleasure in pursuit than in possession.

The day he became champion, his entire life was suddenly changed. With dramatic swiftness he was plunged into a strange world for which he was not prepared. He was hounded by newspaper reporters, by photographers, by autograph seekers, by salesmen, and by old friends who wanted to borrow money. He was besieged to write for newspapers and magazines, to go on the stage, to give lectures, to endorse patent medicines, to help raise money for charity. Hollywood tied him up with a picture contract. He was entertained by the high and mighty both of America and England—entertained by well-educated men who used words he couldn't even understand and who embarrassed him with questions that simply confused him.

"I used to ride a mule to a country school," Jack Dempsey said, as he told me the story. "I took very little interest in my studies and didn't get much of an education, so I didn't know what these educated people were talking about."

Jack Dempsey was so hounded by people that he couldn't even eat in peace. Even if he ordered a meal sent up to his hotel room, six waiters would bring it up instead of one, and then all six of them would stand and stare at him while he ate.

When he arrived in England, Queen Mary issued a royal summons commanding him to appear before her at Buckingham Palace. But Jack Dempsey was so embarrassed that he sent back word he was sick and couldn't come. He is probably the only man in all history who ever refused a royal summons to Buckingham Palace. He really was sick, too—sick with embarrassment, worries, responsibilities, and confusion.

Jack Dempsey won the heavyweight championship from Jess Willard on July 4, 1919. He went to bed late that night, ex-

40

hausted by the celebration that followed his victory, and he had a terrible nightmare. He dreamed that he had been defeated. The dream was so vivid, so real, that he got up, dressed, and dashed downstairs at three o'clock in the morning to buy a newspaper. "I asked one of the newsboys who had won the fight," Jack said.

"Dempsey won," the boy replied. . . . "Say, aren't you Dempsey?"

Jack grinned, embarrassed, and admitted he was Dempsey.

"Well," said the boy, "*you* certainly ought to know who won."

That newsboy would have been amazed if he had known that Jack Dempsey, confused by a nightmare, needed to be assured that he actually was champion of the world.

Dempsey told me that he would never have become a professional fighter at all if he hadn't been so ashamed of his poverty. His father, a happy-go-lucky chap, loved to play the fiddle and was constantly moving from one place to another, looking for adventure and the pot of gold at the end of the rainbow.

One day he loaded his family, his wife, his eleven children, and his fiddle into a covered wagon and started out across the high mountains of Colorado. When they reached a high valley more than ten thousand feet above sea level, the air was so thin and the horses so exhausted that one of them died. There was danger that Jack's mother might die too. She had fainting spells and intense pains. Her husband knew he must get her out of that high altitude at once. He bought a railway ticket and sent her down to her sister's home in Denver. She took Jack with her on the train, hoping the conductor would let him ride free. But Jack was eight years old then, and the conductor vowed that he would put Jack off the train unless his mother paid half-fare. Mrs. Dempsey pleaded that she was desperately ill, that she had no money. But the conductor refused. No money, no ride. The worried mother began to weep.

A cowboy sitting across the aisle called Jack over and said in

41

a low voice, "Tell your mother not to worry, son; if it comes to a showdown, I'll pay your fare."

"I was awfully ashamed of being poor," Dempsey said, as he told me the story. "I resolved fiercely that when I grew up I would never have people insult me and order me to get off a train. I was terribly ashamed of having my mother cry in front of everyone. I resolved right then and there that I would become a great prize fighter and make money, and that someday I would be rich like that cowboy."

Jack Dempsey also resolved that he would become the same kind of a game fighter that his dog was. Jack had a brindle bulldog that he called Denver. That bulldog never fought on the defensive. He never paid any attention to the fact that the other dog was ripping his hide off. "He was an aggressive fighter," Jack said, "and I have always tried to be like him. I have had my lips smashed, my eyes cut, my ribs cracked—but only one of these blows ever really hurt me, and that was the time that John Lester Johnson broke three of my ribs. I never felt any of the other blows, never gave them a second thought. In the ring I kept saying to myself, over and over, 'Nobody is going to stop me. Nobody can really hurt me, I am going to keep hitting the other man no matter what happens.'"

Dempsey also told me some astonishing facts about his fight with Luis Firpo, "The Wild Bull of the Pampas."

Probably no other single event in the history of American sports ever aroused such thrilling, such breath-taking excitement. The great crowd leaped and yelled like madmen. Seventy thousand people paid over a million dollars to see that fight, and no crowd ever saw more action packed into 237 seconds. There were seven knockdowns in the first round—even the sporting writers at the ringside couldn't agree on how many times each man had been knocked down.

Dempsey told me that he had no idea what had happened in that famous fight. He didn't remember that he had knocked

Jack Dempsey

Firpo down several times; didn't even remember that he himself had been knocked clear through the ropes and out of the ring, that he had landed on and wrecked a typewriter, and that he had almost wrecked a couple of sports writers in the crowd.

That fight ended in the second round; but Dempsey said that when he got back to his dressing room, he still had no idea whether the fight had lasted two rounds, or ten rounds, or twenty rounds.

That was the fight for which he was paid over two thousand dollars a second for 237 seconds.

All great athletes have two qualities developed to an astonishing degree: the ability to concentrate and the ability to perform almost automatically. Dempsey says that when he fought, he concentrated so intensely on the fight that he never heard the roars of the crowd, and that his reactions were so quick, so automatic, that he himself frequently didn't know what he was doing. "If you have to stop to figure out what you are going to do, you are too late.

"I used to read the newspapers," he continued, "to find out what had happened in my fights. When I knocked a man down, I would frequently not know what kind of a blow I had hit him. In fact, sometimes I wouldn't even know that I had floored him until I heard the referee counting him out. And when I myself was knocked down, I often wouldn't know how it happened."

Jack Dempsey began to prepare for his ring career when he was only twelve years old. He fitted up an old abandoned chicken house as a gymnasium. He put an old mattress on the floor for tumbling and made a punching bag out of sand and sawdust. He chewed rosin gum all the time to strengthen the muscles of his jaws so he could take a hard punch on the jaw without being hurt.

When it was announced that Jim Jeffries and Jack Johnson were to fight for the heavyweight championship of the world on July 4, 1910, Jack Dempsey was only fifteen years old. But he said to himself, "Someday I am going to whip the man who wins that fight." He took a piece of chalk and drew a picture of Jim Jeffries on one side of his home-made punching bag; and on the other side he drew a picture of Jack Johnson, the Negro fighter. For days he slugged away at both of them. When Jack Johnson won the fight, Dempsey drew Johnson's picture on both sides of the punching bag and whammed away at it.

Nine years later to the day, the little boy who was then punching a home-made bag in a chicken house knocked out the man who knocked out Jack Johnson, and became the heavyweight champion of the world.

Jack Dempsey won the heavyweight championship on July 4, 1919. His father lived in Salt Lake City then, and a Salt Lake newspaper invited him to come down to the paper and get the report of the fight hot off the wires. A large crowd had gathered outside the newspaper office to hear the bulletins. The crowd demanded that Dempsey's father make a speech. He appeared on a balcony and told the crowd that his son couldn't possibly last longer than four rounds, that Jess Willard was too big for him, that Jack didn't stand a chance.

When the news of Jack's victory flashed over the wires, his father rushed out to the balcony and shouted to the crowd: "I told you my boy would win! I told you he would win!"

When training for a bout, Jack Dempsey would pray several times a day; and just before the bell sounded for a fight, he always prayed. That helped him start the fight with confidence and courage.

"I never went to bed in my life and I never ate a meal in my life," he said, "without saying a prayer. I know my prayers have been answered thousands of times, and I know that I never said a prayer in my life without something good coming of it."

HE HATED MATHEMATICS—YET THEY MADE HIM MINISTER OF FINANCE

I AM CONSTANTLY BEING IMPRESSED with the fact that little events that don't seem important when they happen sometimes become turning points in history. For example, four years before the outbreak of the Civil War, during the panic of 1857, a man by the name of Leonard Jerome made six million dollars speculating in Wall Street. That event didn't seem important then to anybody—except to Leonard Jerome. But looking back at it now, we can see that it has had a tremendous effect upon present-day history. Because if that man, Leonard Jerome, hadn't made a fortune speculating in Wall Street, Winston Churchill might never have been born, for that Wall Street speculator, Leonard Jerome, was Winston Churchill's grandfather.

With his six million dollars, Winston Churchill's American grandfather bought a ·part interest in the New York *Times*, founded the first two great racetracks in America, traveled all over the world, and entertained the aristocracy of England. As a result of all this, his American daughter, the beautiful and magnetic Jenny Jerome, met and married Lord Randolph Churchill; and, from this marriage, Winston Churchill was born on November 30, 1874, in one of England's most famous castles —Blenheim Castle.

Winston Churchill is half-American; yet he is probably the most vital and astonishing Englishman now alive.

Biographical Roundup

What a life he has led!

I don't know of any other man on this spinning earth who has packed into his life so much excitement and adventure, so much of the joy and gusto of living. For over a third of a century he has wielded enormous power and influence. In 1911 he was the civilian head of the British Navy, the First Lord of the Admiralty. For over a third of a century he has been molding men and events, and having a rip-roaring good time doing it.

Even as a child Winston Churchill longed to be a soldier, and he often spent an entire day playing with whole regiments of toy soldiers. Later he graduated from the famous military college at Sandhurst in England. He spent years as a professional soldier in the British Army, fighting with the Bengal Lancers in India, fighting with Kitchener in the Sudan desert, fighting the Fuzzy-Wuzzies.

Winston Churchill became famous for his audacity and courage away back in 1900. In fact, his daring and bravery made him so famous that he was elected to Parliament when he was only twenty-six years old.

It happened like this: Back in 1899 he dashed off to South Africa as a war correspondent to report the Boer War for the London *Morning Post* at a salary of 1250 dollars a month, or forty dollars a day. A high price, but he was worth it; for Winston Churchill soon made himself the most famous war correspondent in British history. He not only reported news. He made news by dashing through enemy territory in an armored train which was attacked by cannon fire—made news when he was captured by the Boers and thrown into prison— made news by a sensational escape from the prison camp. The Boers were enraged over his escape because they had lost the most famous prisoner of the war—Winston Churchill, the son of an English Lord.

A huge reward was offered for his capture, dead or alive. After his escape, Churchill traveled hundred of miles through

Winston Churchill

enemy territory in which Boer soldiers stood guard over railroads and bridges. He traveled on foot and on freight trains, sleeping in woods and fields and coal mines, plunging through swamps, and swimming rivers. He tramped across the African plains with hungry vultures flying above him, waiting for him to drop with exhaustion.

The story of his escape was superb. But Winston Churchill knew how to make it breathless. He wrote the story for the *Morning Post* in London—a story tense with drama and suspense, a story that became the journalistic sensation of 1900, a story that all England read with fervor and excitement. England welcomed Winston Churchill home as a national hero. A song was written about his exploits, and enormous crowds gathered to hear him speak; he was elected to Parliament with an enthusiasm inspired by action and glory.

Churchill has long had as his motto, "Never run away from danger." In 1921 he came to America to give a series of forty-five lectures for which he was paid eleven hundred dollars per night. But Scotland Yard discovered that there was grave danger that he would be killed in America. Scotland Yard warned him that a group of bitter men from certain parts of the British Empire had formed in America what Scotland Yard called "Assassination Societies" and that, since Winston Churchill symbolized British authority, he might be shot on his American lecture tour. But in spite of these warnings, Churchill went right ahead with his lecture tour. When he arrived in one western city, he learned that certain members of the "Assassination Society" in that town had already bought tickets for his lecture that night. The city's chief of police was alarmed and ordered the lecture canceled at once; but Churchill's manager, Louis J. Alber, refused to cancel, and Churchill said, "You're right, Alber, one ought never to turn one's back on a threatened danger and try to run away from it. If you do that, you will double the danger. But if you meet it promptly and without

47

flinching, you will reduce the danger by half. Never run away from anything. Never!"

Instead of running away from danger, Winston Churchill frequently ran toward it. When he was made First Lord of the Admiralty, the British Navy had about a half-dozen planes and a half-dozen fliers. That was back in 1911, only eight years after man had flown for the first time. But even in those days, when every flight was a gamble with death, Winston Churchill insisted on flying himself. He piloted his own plane and was in crash after crash, escaping death by inches. The Government urged him to stop flying, but he refused to do so. He loved the thrill and danger of it and was determined to gain first-hand knowledge about flying, for he foresaw even then that planes would revolutionize warfare. Winston Churchill was almost solely responsible for building up the air force of the British Navy.

Another of Winston Churchill's outstanding qualities is his bulldog determination. The way he educated himself is a good example of that. As a young man, he was a very poor scholar. He despised Latin, Greek, mathematics, and French. He passionately believed that one ought first to master English before spending time on foreign languages—and, of course, he was right. But because he despised foreign languages and mathematics, he stood at the very bottom of his class in prep school. And here is an odd fact: this boy who despised mathematics later became Chancellor of the Exchequer and for four years handled Great Britain's finances.

Three times he tried to pass the examinations to get into the royal military college at Sandhurst, and three times he failed. The fourth time he tried, he passed.

Then one day after he had graduated from Harrow and Sandhurst—two of England's most distinguished schools—he discovered what many a college graduate has discovered: namely, that he knew practically nothing. Winston Churchill was twenty-two years old then and an officer in the British Army sta-

48

tioned in India. He thereupon made a high and holy resolution that he would educate himself; so he wrote to his mother in England, begging her to send him biographies, books on history, philosophy, and economics. Then while his fellow-officers slept during the blistering hot afternoons, he devoured with eagerness everything from Plato to Gibbon and Shakespeare. He spent years teaching himself to write the lucid and luminous sentences that march through his speeches and books—sentences that march and sing. From a conspicuously bad speaker with an impediment in his voice, he has transformed himself into one of the most inspiring speakers of all time.

Winston Churchill works from fourteen to seventeen hours a day, frequently seven days a week. He works with tremendous drive and vitality, keeping six secretaries busy. He is still able to do this because he relaxes while he works and rests before he gets tired. He doesn't get out of bed until ten-thirty in the morning; but for three hours before he gets up, he lies propped up in bed, a fat cigar between his teeth, telephoning, dictating letters, and reading newspapers, reports, and cables. After that, he gets up and shaves himself with an old-fashioned razor.

He has lunch at one o'clock, sleeps for an hour, then starts his afternoon schedule. At five o'clock he again climbs into bed, this time for a thirty-minute nap. After dinner he frequently works on until midnight.

A series of Winston Churchill's speeches have been published in a book entitled *While England Slept.* For years, while most British statesmen slept, utterly oblivious to the coming war that was to overwhelm the world, Churchill sensed the grave peril of Hitler. For six years—from 1933 to 1939—he cried out almost every day that Germany was rearming, that Hitler was building tanks and guns and planes, that he planned to bomb Britain and sink the English fleet and conquer the world. He foresaw it all; if England had only listened to his prophetic voice and armed to meet the menace, World War II might still be only a madman's dream.

HE ADVERTISED FOR A WIFE AND GOT
OVER THREE HUNDRED APPLICANTS

A BOOK WAS PUBLISHED in 1943 entitled *Total Peace. What Makes Wars and How to Organize Peace.* It was written by Ely Culbertson, who had devoted four years of his time and enthusiasm to trying to solve the biggest and most tragic problem that you and I face—the problem of preventing future wars.

The New York *Times* called Culbertson's book "a brilliant tour de force both of logic and imagination."

Strangely enough, this Culbertson is the *same* Culbertson who is known to millions of people all over the world as the originator and dramatizer of a system of contract bridge. His system for playing bridge made him rich and famous. But Culbertson has always regarded teaching bridge as a mere sideline. He told me years ago that his real purpose in life was to study mass psychology, to study how men behave as crowds and as nations.

Culbertson's autobiography is a huge book of seven hundred pages entitled *The Strange Lives of One Man.* That title implies that Ely Culbertson has led not one life, but several lives; and that all of these lives have been strange. Strange? The lives he led weren't strange—they were fantastic.

His autobiography is the story of an American millionaire's son who became a Russian revolutionist. He organized a secret Revolutionary Committee among his fellow-students and smuggled into Russia forbidden copies of a Bolshevik newspaper Lenin was publishing in Switzerland.

50

Ely Culbertson

It is the story of a young man who left a luxurious home to live among the poor and to beg for bread on the streets.

Ely Culbertson's life is the story of a man who was brought up by a pious Scottish father to believe that cards were a device of the devil; yet he made himself the most famous card expert of all time.

It is the story of a man who made a million dollars out of teaching bridge; yet he never learned to play cards until he was put in the death house of a Russian jail.

Culbertson's life is the story of an American citizen born in Russia—an American who could speak eight languages, but when he was eighteen years old could speak no more than a hundred words of English; Yale University wouldn't admit him until he had spent months studying English. He attended six famous universities; yet for six years he made his living as a professional gambler.

The *Readers' Digest* described Culbertson as a versatile genius, yet for months he lived the life of a hobo and begged food from housewives who, years later, would have paid money for even his autograph.

To me, one of the most amusing incidents in this incredibly frank autobiography is the story of Culbertson's system for finding his dream girl.

Culbertson told me that he had always been astonished at the haphazard way men went about selecting their wives. And for that matter, who hasn't? A man usually marries some girl he has met quite by chance in school or business or at somebody's home. Culbertson figured he would use the same horse sense in finding a wife that he would use in hiring a stenographer. If he wanted a stenographer, he would advertise in the newspapers in order to have several to choose from. Did he advertise directly for a wife? Oh, no! Nothing so obvious as all that. He was more subtle. He advertised in Italy, posing as an American painter seeking a model. His advertisement specified precisely what he wanted—the exact measurements of the model's waist and hips, the color of her eyes, her complexion, her age, her personality.

Where did he advertise—just any place? No, he made a special trip to the Piedmont region of Italy—a region famous for its beautiful women. He advertised for a model in the city of Turin, under a box number. This was to be a romantic occasion and he was determined to make the most of it. He consulted a psychologist. He not only read, but he studied every book he could find on the art of making love.

His requirements were so exacting that he didn't expect to get more than half a dozen replies. He got over three hundred. The ad stated that the applicant must be between the ages of eighteen and twenty-one. Culbertson told me that many of the women were over forty, with flat feet and bad teeth. The results were both funny and pathetic.

He wrote all three hundred of these would-be artist's models, making appointments to meet them at fifteen-minute intervals on the four corners of the public square. He wrote each girl to look for the man wearing a white rose. As girl after girl came at the appointed time, Culbertson would glance at her and say, "No, signorina, sorry, but I have already engaged a model." That went on hour after hour, day after day, around and around the square: "No signorina . . . no, signorina." Then suddenly he found the girl of his dreams. Nineteen. Gorgeous hair. Wonderful eyes. Personality. Exotic beauty. He wanted to win her love gradually and artistically, so he employed her to give him lessons in the Italian language—hired her to teach him to read Dante's *Divine Comedy*.

Suddenly the courtship ended in comedy—or tragedy—whichever way you want to look at it. For days the police had been watching this Romeo who claimed to be an American painter and interviewed three hundred girls on the corners of the public square. He might have got by with it in peace time, but this happened during the first World War; Culbertson was traveling on an American passport, yet he spoke Italian with a Russian accent. Well, the police figured it just didn't add up, so they grabbed the man who was destined to become world famous as an expert on contract bridge and ordered him to leave Italy immediately. Years later he did find his dream girl in New York City—but he found her without advertising.

Ely Culbertson's father was a Scotsman who loved adventure. He went to Russia and in the Caucasus discovered the main Grozny oil fields, an important part of the rich Russian oil fields that Hitler spent a million lives trying to capture.

Culbertson's father made millions of dollars out of Russian oil and married the daughter of a Cossack General.

Ely Culbertson is half-American and half-Russian. His father wanted his son educated in America, so he sent him to Yale. But Ely was shocked and disappointed at Yale. He had but recently felt the bloody lashes of Czarist soldiers. They had jailed him for his revolutionary activity and had killed his Russian sweetheart. He had seen too much of life and death in Russia to become a Yale freshman.

After spending four months at New Haven, he turned his monthly allowance of 125 dollars over to his brother and announced that he was going to live in the slums in New York. "I wanted to know," Culbertson said to me, "how the lowest classes of America lived. I wanted to live as they lived." He spent the next three years doing just that. Why? Because he was passionately determined to become a great writer and he knew that one cannot become a great writer by merely studying books. To be a writer, one must live intensely, know human nature, and have something to write about.

Culbertson was determined to study at first hand the rough and tumble of American life. For months this millionaire's son lived with thieves and dope peddlers and gangsters of New York's Bowery. He lived for a while in cheap rooming houses where drunks and down-and-outers could sleep for ten cents a night.

He worked for a while as a helper in a saloon. Later he made his living by selling newspapers on the Bowery. He made enough to buy a plate of beans, a cup of tea, and to spend twenty cents for a bed in the Newsboy Lodging House where Horatio Alger had once lived. He attended night school at Cooper Union; he stood in bread lines; he lived with a dope-fiend.

Months later he got a job acting as a timekeeper for a gang of laborers who were building the Canadian National Railway through the Canadian Rockies. With fiery oratory, he told them they were being cheated and underpaid by the contractors and robbed by the company stores. He organized a strike and won higher wages for the men, but he got himself kicked out of the company's employ.

After walking two hundred miles to the nearest town, he sent every dollar he had to a bank in San Francisco and decided to bum his way to the Pacific coast. He stole rides on freight cars, associated with hobos, and begged food from door to door. He washed dishes in Montana, planted corn in Oregon, and picked fruit in California—and everywhere he went he studied people, studied life.

In Berkeley, California, he spent six months studying the literature of anarchy; then suddenly gave up reading about revolutions and rushed down to Mexico to join a real revolt that had broken out there. He was captured and thrown into jail, and only his American passport kept him from being shot.

Culbertson's father had invested all his fortune in the gold bonds of the Imperial Government of Russia. When the Czar was overthrown and Lenin established a Soviet Republic in Russia, all of the millions of dollars that Culbertson's father had invested in Russian bonds weren't worth a postage stamp.

In 1921 Culbertson's father applied for a job as night watchman in New York City. Ely Culbertson tried to get a job teach-

54

ing philosophy and sociology, but he failed.

He tried selling coal, and failed. Then he tried selling coffee, but he failed at that, too. Finally, he gave private lessons in French literature to a group of socialists in New York, and acted as concert manager for his brother, a violinist.

It never occurred to him then to try to teach bridge. He was a poor card player, and he asked so many questions and held so many post-mortem examinations that no one wanted to play with him. He read books about bridge, but they didn't help much, so he started to write a book himself. He wrote four books. They were worthless and he knew it. He tore up the manuscripts before they were ever put in type.

But he let nothing discourage him and he persevered until he developed a system which became the most widely known contract bridge system in the world. His bridge books have been translated into a dozen languages and have sold over a million copies.

Ely Culbertson told me that the greatest satisfaction he has yet found in his strange tumultuous life, he found during the four years he spent preparing *Total Peace,* his plan to prevent future wars.

And so Culbertson, the bridge expert, may make a vital contribution to our effort to preserve lasting peace.

HIS PARENTS WERE SERFS, BUT HE NOW RULES TWO HUNDRED MILLION PEOPLE

THE MOST POWERFUL INDIVIDUAL on earth today is a man who is worshipped by millions of people and hated by still other millions. His parents were once serfs—practically slaves—who were literally bought and sold with the land on which they lived. But this son of two former serfs now rules over one-sixth of all the land on this earth. In his hands he holds the power of life and death over two hundred million people.

You may admire him or you may despise him; but one thing is certain—you cannot ignore him. I do not see how anyone can fail to respect his lifelong loyalty to a single purpose: to give his country to the people and to fit his people to run their country and enjoy doing it.

His name is Stalin—Joseph Stalin. This is not his real name, of course. His real name is Iosif Vissarionovitch Dzugashvili.

Stalin was born in 1879, down near the Russian oil fields, in a tiny little house, facing on an alley, that rented for a dollar and a half a month, or a nickel a day.

Stalin comes from Georgia, which lies between the Black and the Caspian Seas. The Georgians still speak their own language even though their land has been a part of Russia for 140 years. Stalin spoke Georgian until he was twenty years old. The language is as different from Russian as Spanish is from English. Stalin still speaks Russian with a Georgian accent.

Czar Alexander II abolished serfdom in Russia three years

Joseph Stalin

before America abolished slavery. When little Joe Stalin was born in 1879, his mother and father were free—free, that is, to take in washing and to repair shoes for their daily bread.

Let's see how Joseph Stalin made himself autocratic ruler of all the vast lands that had been dominated by the haughty Czars of Russia for five hundred years. Let's see if we can figure out how Iosif Vissarionovitch Dzugashvili became Joseph Stalin, a one-man world power of the first rank.

First, he got an education that lifted him out of his drab, poverty-ridden environment and gave him vision and purpose. Stalin's father wanted his son to become a shoemaker. But his mother dreamed dreams, as all mothers do. This untutored woman who was born in virtual slavery, this woman who had to wash and sew for a living, longed to have her son live in a brighter, better world than she had ever known. She often went to the Russian Orthodox Church and burned candles before the altar of some saint and knelt and wept as she prayed that her son Iosif would become a priest. She didn't care how long she worked nor how hard. She was working for a cause, a holy cause.

Somehow she obtained a scholarship for her son in a Theological Seminary in Tiflis. Stalin attended this training school for priests for several years. Then one day, when he was fifteen years old, something happened. In itself it was a simple thing, yet it was to have repercussions that would some day shake the world. It was merely this: Stalin got hold of a book that has done more to change the history of the world than any other non-religious book ever written—Karl Marx's *Capital, or a Critique of Political Economy.*

Stalin was so stirred by this book that he immediately plunged into the secret activities of the followers of Karl Marx. He was so stirred that he resolved to devote his life to fighting for the interests of his people. He rebelled at the dreadful poverty in which tens of millions of Russian peasants lived—a poverty so

57

extreme that it is almost impossible for us Americans even to conceive of it. Many Russian peasants couldn't afford to buy salt with which to season their food.

Stalin believed that the only way to improve the living conditions of the peasants and workers was by revolution.

Because of his revolutionary activities, Stalin was expelled from the training school for priests. Through the next quarter of a century he worked tirelessly for his ideals. He was even willing to live the life of a hunted animal. For years he had no home. For weeks at a time he would spend each night in a different place. For the sake of his ideals, he spent eight years in prison.

But always during these years of hardship, flight, and capture he was working for the Party—delivering revolutionary speeches, and editing a revolutionary newspaper in a cellar in St. Petersburg.

Stalin was the kind of a revolutionist who was willing to risk not only his freedom, but also his very life—week after week, year after year. After the Revolution of 1905 failed, Lenin and Trotsky fled to Switzerland to save their necks. But not Stalin. No, Joe Stalin remained in Russia and defied the Czar's police at a time when capture meant that he might be backed up against a wall and shot.

When Lenin was in exile, he smuggled into Russia articles written on cigarette papers, or enclosed in tin cans which were hidden in barrels of wine. Stalin printed these in his underground paper.

Six times Stalin was exiled to Siberia, and five times he escaped and returned to his regular job of fomenting revolution. Iron bars and whips and threats of death—none of these things could swerve Stalin. They merely deepened his one passion: to overthrow the autocratic government of his country and to give Russia's land and wealth to the people. The last time—the sixth time—that the Czar's police caught up with Stalin, they took no

Joseph Stalin

chances. They put two guards over him and exiled him to a place from which few prisoners ever returned, a tiny frozen settlement of three huts, located in Siberia, only eighteen miles south of the Arctic Circle. There was no need of a prison there. If Stalin had tried to escape, he would have died of cold and hunger. For four years he lived in that dreaded, starvation-stricken section of the Siberian Steppes. Food is so scarce there that the Russians say: "In the Steppes even a bug is meat." If he wanted fire wood, he had to go out in the forest and cut it. He couldn't read or study—it was too cold. He had to do hard physical work to keep from freezing to death.

Hopeless as his condition seemed, Stalin never gave up. He believed that some day, somehow, he would escape. With the Revolution of 1917, he did escape. He was released.

The name Stalin comes from the Russian word *stal* which means *steel,* and his spirit was as hard to bend as a sheet of cold steel.

It was Stalin, probably more than any other man, who held the Bolshevik Party together during these years and made possible the revolution that finally overthrew the Czar's cruel and dictatorial government.

Stalin has been married twice. His first wife, Catherine, was a young girl with little education. She bore him a son. Their married life was pathetic. Stalin was a revolutionist, hunted by the police. He didn't dare remain home for more than a few days at a time before dashing off in the darkness. Four years after their marriage, Catherine died of tuberculosis.

Stalin did not marry again until he was nearly forty, and then he married a girl of seventeen—a girl less than half his age. She died twelve years ago from blood poisoning brought on by a ruptured appendix. She was buried, contrary to all Soviet practice, with a showy and almost Orthodox religious burial.

This girl wife bore Stalin a son and a daughter. Both of his sons are serving the fighting forces of Russia. The older son is a captain of artillery; the younger, in the air force, has been decorated for bravery.

As the supreme ruler of Russia, Stalin lives near the Royal Palace where the Czars lived for sixty-nine years. He could, if he desired, live in huge rooms amidst immortal paintings and priceless tapestries and sleep in beds where the mighty Czars rested. Yet Joseph Stalin lives in a small four-room apartment that was once occupied by a servant of the Czar.

His food comes from the Kremlin kitchen and is served by a soldier. It is the same food that is served to hundreds of officers who work in the Kremlin.

Stalin never makes himself conspicuous, never tries to show off. He is embarrassed by strangers. Ambassadors of great nations have spent years in Moscow without ever once seeing Stalin.

Stalin dresses fastidiously. He loves fine materials, delicate weaves, and pastel shades. The late Wendell Willkie met Stalin four or five times. Stalin never dressed quite the same on any of these occasions. One day his tunic would be pale pastel blue, while his riding trousers, encased in shiny black boots, would be salmon pink. The next day, he would have on still other colors.

When visitors compliment Stalin on the miracles he has accomplished, he merely says: "It is nothing compared to what we are going to do."

Stalin, mighty as he is, has the good sense to realize that he is not infallible. He once wrote: "The main thing is to have the courage to admit one's errors and to have the strength to correct them in the shortest possible time."

Stalin gets things done, but his methods are often ruthless. Even Lenin, the father of the Russian Revolution, said, in speaking of Stalin: "This cook will make too hot a stew." Well, if this Russian cook, Joe Stalin, had not made a boiling hot stew for Hitler and his Nazis, can you imagine how many more

60

American soldiers would have had to sacrifice their lives to conquer Hitler?

For Joe Stalin, the dictator, while intending merely to save Russia, has also done a lot to save democracy and to save you and me. It is terrifying to think what might have happened to us had it not been for the heroic sacrifices of the Red Armies of Joseph Stalin.

HE ONCE WAS AFRAID OF GIRLS—NOW THEY STOP WORK FOR HALF A DAY JUST TO CATCH A GLIMPSE OF HIM

CLARK GABLE IS PROBABLY the most widely known individual who ever served in the American Army. One of the greatest motion picture personalities of our time, he is known and admired by countless millions of picture fans in China, India, Africa, Europe and South America—millions who know practically nothing of American military leaders or American history.

When Clark Gable visited South America years ago, women threw their arms around him and clung to his neck. They grabbed his hat, tore off his coat, and ripped his shirt to pieces —for souvenirs.

When he joined the Army, he avoided motion picture shows and all glamour spots and tried to keep himself hidden; but a group of admiring women in England chased him into a church; and a group of girls who were helping to harvest crops on farms in England stopped work for half a day to hang around an American Army base, hoping to catch a glimpse of their hero.

Clark Gable was forty-two when he enlisted in the Army in 1942. In order to join the Army, he tore up one of the best contracts ever signed in Hollywood—a contract that guaranteed to pay him 7500 dollars a week for forty weeks out of each year for a period of seven years. That meant he got as much in ten weeks as the President of the United States gets in an entire year.

Clark Gable

Yes, he exchanged a contract that guaranteed him almost a third of a million dollars a year for a khaki uniform and fifty dollars a month.

A few years ago I had the pleasure of interviewing Clark Gable. He is friendly, modest, unassuming. I liked him immensely.

On several occasions, he has been selected as one of the ten best-dressed men in America. When I interviewed him in his dressing room, he had a turkish towel around his neck and he was using the top of a cold cream jar for an ash tray.

Clark Gable has played many dramatic roles in pictures, but no fiction story that he has ever portrayed on the screen is as interesting and dramatic as the actual story of his own life.

When he was fifteen, he stopped late one night at a lunch wagon in Akron, Ohio, to get a ham sandwich and a cup of coffee. That little event changed his entire life. Why? Because in that lunch wagon he met a group of actors who were playing in a stock company in Akron. Clark Gable was enchanted by these actors. He had come to Akron a few months previously and had gotten a job as a timekeeper in a rubber factory; but all of his life before that had been spent on a farm, milking the cows, feeding the hogs, pitching hay, and plowing corn—hard grinding labor that he despised.

Now, for the first time, Clark Gable had met actors. He was so excited with the life they led that he tried to get a job behind the footlights himself. That was impossible, but he did get a job as a callboy in the theater. His job was to get the actors out of their dressing rooms and onto the stage at the right moment; in addition, he ran errands for the actors, took their laundry out, sewed buttons on their costumes, and helped them in every way he could.

He worked in that theater as a callboy for two years. And how much salary do you suppose he got? The answer is he got nothing—nothing but experience—for those two years of work.

63

How did he manage to live? He slept on a cot back stage and used his overcoat for a blanket.

How did he eat? Well, the actors liked him so much that they invited him to eat with them twice a day.

In those days he had to form the habit of skipping breakfast; years later, when he was world-famous and was making millions, he still continued to eat only two meals a day.

Skipping breakfast? He didn't mind that. He didn't mind the hardships because he was fifteen and doing what he longed to do: living in a dream world, a world of make believe—a world of footlights, grease paint, applause, and romance. He was probably happier than any millionaire in Ohio.

I asked Clark Gable if he was any happier when he was making a thousand dollars a day than he was when he was a callboy in the theater working for nothing. He replied, "No. Money and fame don't bring happiness."

After two years at the Akron theater, tragedy suddenly struck. His stepmother died. That death broke up his father's home, and it also broke up Clark Gable's plans for the future.

His father announced that he was going to leave the farm and go down to Oklahoma to work in the oil fields, and he decided to take his son with him. The old man was disgusted. Imagine having a worthless son who worked two years in a theater for nothing when he could be making twelve dollars a day in the oil fields. The old man issued an order. There was to be no argument. No back talk. So for the next two years Clark Gable, grimy and greasy from head to foot all day long, swung an eighteen-pound sledge hammer, climbed oil well derricks sixty feet high to grease the crown blocks, and worked in the refineries.

Finally, when he was nineteen, Clark put his foot down. He vowed that he was going back to his dreams—back to the theater. He joined a traveling show called "The Jewell Players." It was a third-rate tent show, operating on a shoestring.

Clark Gable

The troupe journeyed from one small town to another in Kansas, Nebraska, and the Middle West, pitching their tent in vacant lots and charging five, ten, and fifteen cents to see performances of *Uncle Tom's Cabin,* or *Charley's Aunt.*

I asked Clark Gable what salary he got with this traveling show. He laughed. Nobody got any salary. They paid their bills—if they could—and then divided the profits—if there were any to divide. He recalled that he once got two dollars and seventy cents as his share of a week's profits.

Finally on March 21, 1922, the company found itself stranded in Butte, Montana, in a blizzard—stranded with no cash, no prospects, no hope—nothing but debts and disappointments.

The next morning Gable drifted down to the railway station. He was hungry and cold. His pants were patched, his shoes had holes in the bottom, and he didn't have a dime. In fact his total cash assets were exactly seven cents. He wrote out a telegram to his father saying he would come home if his father would wire him the money. After writing the telegram, Clark Gable hesitated. He stood staring out into the snow storm with unseeing eyes, thinking, wondering. Should he send the telegram or not?

Should he give up the work he loved for something he despised? He realized he was standing at the crossroads of life and making a decision that would have a profound effect upon his future. Finally, with the dogged determination characteristic of the Dutch (both his mother and father were Pennsylvania Dutch), he resolved to pursue his career. He tore up the telegram, walked out of the station, jumped on a freight train, and rode out of town like a hobo.

When the train reached the Snake River Valley, a brakeman discovered Gable in a box car. That was back in 1922. Twelve years later Clark Gable was destined to be one of the best known men on earth. But the brakeman didn't know that and he kicked him off the train. Clark had to work in a lumber camp for three months to get enough money to pay his fare to Portland, Oregon.

When he did reach Portland, he joined another traveling stock company. That one also went on the rocks, and again Clark Gable had to make his living as a day laborer—carrying chains for a group of surveyors, driving a team of mules in the hop fields, cutting brush for road builders, working in a lumber mill.

When he got back to Portland the second time, he found it almost impossible to secure work. The jobs he wanted were always filled by the time he applied for them; so he showed his initiative and originality by getting a job working for the want-ad department of a newspaper. His job was to classify the want-ads before they were published. This enabled him to pick out the precise job he wanted and land it before it was advertised in the paper. The job he selected was working as a lineman for the telephone company at sixteen dollars a week.

That job was to mark another turning point in his life. One day he was sent over to the Little Theater in Portland to fix a telephone that was out of order. While fixing the telephone he got acquainted with the stage director, Josephine Dillon.

He took lessons in acting from her, courted her, and married her. That was December, 1924. But many more discouraging, heart-breaking years were to pass before he would play the part of a gangster in a picture that would start him on the way to stardom, a picture called *A Free Soul*.

During those years he played small parts on Broadway and hung around Hollywood, living in hall bedrooms, eating in cheap restaurants, visiting the casting offices of the picture studios, looking for work—any kind of work—month after month, year after year, with no encouragement. Finally, he did get a speaking part in a picture. His hopes soared. Surely he would get a toe-hold in Hollywood now. But he was wrong. Six years passed before he got another speaking part in pictures, and it didn't amount to much.

Once during those eight years he got a job working as an extra in the chorus of a Hollywood production of *The Merry Widow*. His pay was seven dollars and a half a day. Years later, when he became world-famous, Clark Gable had that notice of his seven-fifty-a-day part in *The Merry Widow* framed and hung on the walls of his studio. Across the notice he wrote: "Just to remind you, Gable. Just to remind you."

But Clark Gable will never have to worry about taking himself too seriously. He has too much horse-sense for that. When he attended the Army Air Corps School at Miami, he was voted the most popular man in the school because he was likeable, honest, down-to-earth, and didn't put on airs.

For months he trained to be a gunner in a Flying Fortress— a training that washes out tens of thousands of younger men. But it didn't wash out Clark Gable at forty-two.

Clark Gable became one of the most famous lovers on the screen, yet he told me that as a young man he was almost a total failure with the girls. Boy-like, he was always in love with some girl, but he said that most of them never knew anything about it because he didn't have the courage to tell them. He said he always envied the boys who could step up and talk to the girls without blushing.

He may have been afraid of the girls then, but he certainly has courage of the highest order now—courage and skill that won him the Air Medal for "exceptionally meritorious achievement while participating in five separate bomber missions over occupied Continental Europe." The citation declares that "the courage, coolness and skill displayed by Captain Gable on these occasions reflect great credit upon him."

THEY HIRED HIM TO TEACH SCHOOL
BECAUSE HE COULD FIGHT

DURING THE FIRST WORLD WAR a man who had been a school teacher in Louisiana tried to join our Air Force. But his first application was rejected with this written comment: "Does not possess necessary qualifications to be successful aviator."

Later that man came to be regarded as one of our greatest geniuses in combat aviation. His name is Chennault—Major-General Claire Lee Chennault. Within thirty days after Pearl Harbor, his air force of volunteer American pilots in China, pitifully small as it was, stopped the Jap Air Force and sent their bombers flaming down into the jungles of Burma. The General and his American volunteer pilots, "The Flying Tigers," won the *only* victories the Allied nations won over Japan during the tragic six months that followed Pearl Harbor.

Remember the unbroken disastrous defeats that we met during those tragic six months? During that time the Japs conquered the Philippines, the Dutch East Indies, and Singapore; sank two of Great Britain's mightiest battleships, the *Prince of Wales* and the *Repulse;* conquered American territory in the Aleutians; and were on the verge of invading Australia.

The only bright spots in the picture for us during those months of disaster were the victories of Chennault and his Flying Tigers. The odds against them were incredible, but so were the Flying Tigers. They won victories that still make us gasp with astonishment. They wrote in blood and fire over the

68

skies of Burma a record that has never been equaled in the history of combat aviation.

When the Japs struck at Pearl Harbor, General Chennault had about fifty trained pilots and slightly more than a hundred obsolete planes. He was so hard up for spare parts that after a battle he would send Chinese coolies out into the jungle to recover bits of Jap planes and motors that he might use to patch up his own ships. As for gasoline—well, all gasoline had to be flown in from India over some of the world's highest mountains. It was so scarce that its movements were recorded as carefully as shipments of gold.

In the ninety days following Pearl Harbor, Chennault's Flying Tigers were outnumbered twenty to one, and they rarely had enough ammunition to last longer than sixty seconds of firing, yet they destroyed twenty Jap planes for every one they lost; and they killed ninety-two Jap pilots for every pilot they lost—a record of air war that may stand for centuries.

The Japs got their first shock when they tried to bomb the Burma Road on December 23, 1941, only sixteen days after Pearl Harbor. Suddenly the Flying Tigers—six of them flying in three pairs—broke through the clouds and darted downwards turning and twisting and flashing through the sky. Then they let loose a spurt of fire and down plunged all but one of the Jap bombers in a mass of flames. Nothing like it had ever happened before in the five years that the insolent Japs had dominated the air over China.

That was only the beginning. Forty-eight hours later, on Christmas Day, Jap planes bombed Rangoon, killing sixteen hundred civilians. Eighteen of the Flying Tigers tore into the Jap bombers, blasting nineteen of them to pieces, and not one American plane or pilot was lost.

The Flying Tigers had tasted blood now. The next day at dawn they destroyed an entire unit of Japanese bombers hidden in the jungles of Thaïland, destroyed them before they

69

could get off the ground. That night they struck again, wiping out another gang of Japanese air raiders.

The war lords of Tokyo had their buck teeth rattled. In four bloody days they had lost more planes over Burma than they had lost in an entire year over China.

General Chennault and his men helped to shoot the Jap invasion schedule full of holes. They helped to keep thousands of Japanese soldiers waiting in the steaming jungles of Burma for an air force that never arrived; and they helped to keep the Japs from invading India. If the Japs had invaded India, only a few hundred miles, they would have captured Calcutta and the biggest steel mills in the British Empire.

What kind of a man is Major-General Claire Chennault? What is the secret of his incredible success against the Jap planes? He was brought up in a way that most parents would not approve. His mother died when he was four. His father, who was busy running a cotton farm and acting as sheriff, believed that the way to develop self-reliance in a country boy was to throw him on his own and let him run wild. So young Claire did just that, with little more restraint than a wild animal. To be sure, he did attend a country school off and on, but he studied there only the subjects that he liked—principally geography and history.

The one activity that really fired his imagination and shaped his character was reading the adventures of Daniel Boone, Tom Sawyer, and Huckleberry Finn. He became so excited, so thrilled, that he resolved that he, too, would live as Daniel Boone and Huckleberry Finn had lived. He would disappear into the deep tangled woods of Louisiana for a week at a time, carrying a gun and fishing tackle and matches, and live on the fish he caught and the wild turkeys he shot.

Wasting time? No, he was filling his youthful days with the gusto of high adventure and was developing the very qualities that helped to make him the inspired military leader that he is

70

today—qualities of initiative, courage, originality, quick thinking, and straight shooting.

And speaking of shooting, he decided to go to West Point. But getting into West Point meant passing stiff examinations. To get ready, he started studying at Louisiana State University. But his plans were wrecked by a tiny insect rolling up from Mexico. The boll weevil destroyed half the cotton crop on his father's plantation and forced Claire Chennault to earn his own living. He tried to get a job in business, but failed. He resolved to become a schoolteacher and he got his first job as such, not because of his scholastic standing, but because of his ability to fight. One day while he was attending Louisiana State, the battleship *Mississippi* was anchored in the Mississippi River opposite the University. The sailors from the battleship painted the town red and then challenged the university boys to a fight. Claire agreed to fight any middleweight boxer on the battleship. He hadn't the faintest idea at the time that the champion middleweight fighter of the entire Navy was on that battleship. Chennault fought him for ten rounds with gloves on, and then challenged the champion to take off the gloves and fight another ten rounds with bare fists. The champ refused, and the University roared with pride. The news of this astonishing fight traveled fast. It reached a country school where the boys were so ornery that they had whipped every teacher that had been assigned to teach them. Claire Chennault was hired to teach that school. He had to knock some of the bullies down and bloody their noses, but he did teach them readin' and writin' an' 'rithmetic. He succeeded where other teachers had failed.

When the first World War broke out, he walked out of the schoolroom and joined the Army. When the war ended he was a lieutenant in the air service of the regular Army. Even then he had the vision to see how future wars would be fought; and as the years went by he protested violently against the inadequate methods being used by the Air Force. For years he stud-

71

ied and experimented constantly, and then he wrote a book entitled *The Role of Defensive Pursuit.* His superiors denounced him as a visionary and a radical and retired him when he was forty-six years of age. The reason given was that his hearing had been impaired by the roar of motors in open-cockpit planes.

A few months later he was made Air Advisor to General Chiang Kai-shek in China.

In the summer of 1941 he toured the flying fields of the United States, urging American pilots to join him in China. The pay? Six hundred dollars a month. On top of that, the Chinese Government paid a bounty of five hundred dollars for each Jap plane shot down. One hundred American pilots who were spoiling for a fight followed him back to the Orient—one hundred against the entire Japanese Air Force.

General Chennault had already spent four years in China psychoanalyzing the Jap pilots, memorizing their fighting rules, and learning their reactions to an endless series of combat conditions. He would often peer at the sky through a pair of field glasses and describe to an open-mouthed audience of pilots each detailed move that an attacking Japanese squadron would make before it actually made it.

He required American volunteer flyers to practice each flying maneuver six hours a day until it was perfect. Then he trained them to execute these maneuvers in groups. The General knew that the Jap Zero planes could fly faster and turn quicker than the heavier P-40 Tomahawks the Americans were flying—but that the P-40's could dive faster and hit harder. He trained his men to attack in teams, in wide weaving strokes from above and below, and to avoid dog fights. "After you strike, fly home," he warned his men. "Don't stop to see what happens next—it might happen to you!"

In a few months Chennault hammered this group into the most amazing air force the world had ever seen—an air force that, often outnumbered twenty to one, stood off the entire Japanese Air Force in southeastern Asia.

The Flying Tigers were taken over by the United States Army in 1942; and General Chennault was made Commander of the 14th Air Force in China.

We owe to General Claire Lee Chennault an eternal debt of gratitude for delaying the Japanese those precious months after Pearl Harbor—delaying them until we were ready to strike back.

HE ONCE BUILT KITES ON THE KITCHEN FLOOR IN KANSAS—NOW HE BUILDS BOMBERS IN HIS OWN FACTORY

On January 15, 1886, Mrs. Minta Martin, a housewife in Macksburg, Iowa, had a dream. She dreamed that she was flying through the air in a flying machine. She dreamed that she flew all over her home town of Macksburg, waved to her friends in the street below, and felt sorry for them because they couldn't fly, too.

That dream occurred seventeen years before the Wright brothers made their first flight.

Under ordinary circumstances, Mrs. Martin probably would have paid no attention to this dream; but she was about to become a mother, and she had often heard people talk about the meaning of dreams. When her son, Glenn Martin, was born two days later, she interpreted the dream to mean that some day her son would fly through the air just as she had done.

The strange part of the story is that her boy did learn to fly shortly after the Wright brothers did. In fact he was the third man in America to fly in a machine built by the flyer himself.

Today Martin is the dean of the aviation industry and has made aeronautical history in a fabulous manner. His factory, the Glenn L. Martin Company, near Baltimore, Maryland, is one of the world's three largest builders of aircraft. He has built the Marauder bombers for the Army, the Mariner bombers for the Navy, and the Baltimore bombers for the British. He is the world's largest builder of flying boats. Yet it is entirely possible that Glenn Martin might never have entered the aviation industry if his mother had not felt that her dream revealed he was destined to fly.

Why do I say that? Because as he grew up, his mother told him about her dream and created in her son a confidence, a vision, an ambition to conquer the winds. And there was an almost constant gale of wind to conquer on the prairies of southwest Kansas, where Glenn spent his boyhood.

When I interviewed him, he told me that the winds of Kansas played a vital part in his boyhood. When he was a child of six, Glenn Martin took one of his mother's bed sheets, made a sail out of it, fastened it to his little red wagon and let the wind drive him and his wagon down the street. Later he put on a pair of skates, held a home-made sail in his hands, and let the wind drive him across the ice. He even used a sail to drive his bicycle. Martin says he cannot remember a time when he was not fascinated by sailing surfaces.

When Mrs. Minta Martin was living in southwest Kansas many years ago, I doubt that she had ever heard the word *psychology;* but when I interviewed her, she told me how she helped her son to develop courage and self-confidence. Modern psychologists surely would approve the technique she used. She gave her son all the responsibility he could carry and she gave it to him as early as he could carry it. When he wanted a pair of skates and didn't have the money to buy them, his mother urged him to go to a blacksmith's shop and make his own skates; and he did. When he wanted his mother to buy him a kite, she urged him to make his own kite; and he did. In fact, Glenn Martin made a new kind of kite that he had read about in a boys' magazine—a box kite, or biplane kite. He made his own box kite on the kitchen floor and was thrilled to discover that it could fly up straighter and higher than any other kite in the skies of Kansas.

He was so proud of his achievement that he organized a kite-flying contest and carried off all the honors himself. The result? Just this: the other boys in town urged him to make box kites for them. Little Glenn Luther Martin, who was destined, fifty years later, to make the largest flying boat in the world—the *Mars*—started a kite factory in his mother's kitchen, turning out three kites a night and selling them for a quarter each—ten cents down and five cents a week.

His self-confidence mounted and soared because he discovered that he had a mechanical gift, that he could do things other boys couldn't do.

Thirty years later a Cleveland newspaper man asked Martin, who was then manufacturing bombers that sank battleships, how he got his start as a plane manufacturer. Glenn Martin replied, "My mother influenced me most. She encouraged me to make kites on the kitchen floor. She encouraged me to believe in myself."

When the first automobiles came to Kansas, Martin was eager to master the strange horseless carriage. He got a job in a garage. Later, when his family moved to Santa Ana, California, he started a garage of his own obtaining the agency for the Ford and Maxwell automobiles in his territory. By the time he was twenty years old, he was making from three to four thousand dollars a year selling and repairing automobiles.

Then suddenly something happened that changed the entire course of his life.

One day in 1905 Glenn Martin read a newspaper article that startled him and fascinated him—an article reporting that the Wright brothers, at Kitty Hawk, North Carolina, had soared through the air in a flying machine for one hundred seconds. He was greatly excited by the report, because he realized even then that the flying machine was thundering in a new era.

So the Wright brothers had flown for one hundred seconds, had they? Taking out his watch, Martin counted one hundred

Glenn L. Martin

seconds. "Why, if man can stay in the air for one hundred seconds now," he said to himself, "the time will come when we can build flying machines that will stay in the air an hour—maybe five, ten hours—who knows?"

A few months later he got excited again—excited over a picture of the Wright brothers' flying machine that he found in a technical magazine. After studying that picture, he said to his mother, "Why this is just a big kite with an engine in it. I can build kites, and I can build engines, so I am going to build one of these airplanes and fly it myself." "Yes, son," his mother replied, as she thought of the dream she had had two nights before he was born. "Yes, son," she said, "you can do it."

Glenn Martin was twenty years old then and was so thrilled about flying that he wanted to devote all his time to it. He couldn't, because he had to make a living. By day he ran a garage and sold Ford and Maxwell cars; but at night—ah, when night came, he did what he really wanted to do! First, he built a glider—a sort of huge, man-carrying kite—and learned to soar in this glider without an engine. After experimenting for months with it, he was eager to build a real plane, a plane powered by a gasoline engine. But how could he? He knew little or nothing about the science of aerodynamics and had never had any technical training whatever.

Now here he was trying to build an airplane, without blueprints, without any guidance whatever from anyone. He was so desperate for help that he finally went to the public library and read a book on bridge construction, hoping desperately that, somehow, by studying the strains and stresses of bridges he would get some idea about how to solve the problems of strains and stresses in a flimsy airplane that had to carry a man and an engine.

Glenn Martin built that first airplane of his in an abandoned Southern Methodist church in Santa Ana, California, in 1908. He rented the abandoned church for twelve dollars a month.

His father was ashamed of the fact that Glenn Martin was such a crackpot. He was ashamed of having a son wasting his time trying to build an airplane when he could be out making money selling cars. The other young men in town sneered at Glenn Martin because he spent all his nights and even his holidays building a flying machine. One old lady pleaded with Glenn Martin's mother to make her son "stop having dealings with the Devil. If God had intended man to fly," she said, "God would have given him wings."

The only person who gave Glenn any encouragement whatever was his mother. She remembered her dream. She knew her boy would fly. She worked in the abandoned church with him every night, holding the coal-oil lamp so that he could see what he was working on. People stared in at the windows to see what the crazy fool was doing. He painted the windows. He padlocked the doors. But still they came and still they laughed. He had to hire a guard to keep them away.

For thirteen months Glenn Martin and his mother worked building that plane—worked nights and on the Fourth of July and Christmas Day and New Year's Day. But don't feel sorry for him. It wasn't really work. It was excitement. He wasn't merely building an airplane. He was conquering the winds. He was making a dream come true. He was probably getting far more fun out of life than any millionaire or king on earth. Glenn Martin told me that the thirteen months he spent building his first plane were the most enjoyable months of his life.

He installed a twelve-horsepower automobile engine in his plane. To save weight, he took off the cast-iron crankcase and made one of light copper. He had to whittle out six propellers before he finally got one that worked.

Finally the airplane was finished. The end of the church had been torn out, and at midnight, on the last day of July, 1909, Glenn Martin and his two helpers wheeled the flimsy machine out of the church and pushed and pulled it for three miles up

Glenn L. Martin

the road to a field where it was to be tested out the next morning. The strange machine was pushed up the road at midnight so it wouldn't scare any horses.

Just as dawn was breaking on August 1, 1909, Glenn Martin climbed into his home-made airplane and started the engine. It sputtered and coughed. He increased the power. The flimsy plane shook and trembled and lurched—and then a miracle happened: it left the ground! Glenn L. Martin, the boy who used to make kites on the kitchen floor back in Kansas, was actually flying! That was the greatest thrill of his life.

Glenn Martin built the China Clippers, the first flying boats to span the vast Pacific, and many of America's great wartime flying boats.

Glenn Martin's life is a striking illustration of the power of persistence and singleness of purpose. He recently said: "If you decide on a course and if, when the going gets thick, you don't lose sight of your objective, then you are bound to get somewhere."

THE GREAT-GRANDSON OF QUEEN VICTORIA IS THE TOUGHEST COMMANDO OF THEM ALL

TENS OF THOUSANDS OF American boys fought out in the Far East under the leadership of a cousin of the King of England and a great-grandson of Queen Victoria. Probably the handsomest, most romantic, and most colorful leader in World War II, yet, he is a rootin', tootin', hell-for-leather scrapper if there ever was one. His name is Mountbatten. His intimate friends call him "Dickie," but his full name is Lord Louis Francis Albert Victor Nicholas Mountbatten. He is the Supreme Commander of Allied Forces in Southeast Asia. His command covers about one-twelfth of the earth's surface.

Lord Louis Mountbatten was given this command because he is a specialist in naval transportation. Secretary of War Stimson congratulated Mountbatten on his "stinging defeat" of an ambitious Jap task force in the jungle country north of Akyab—Japan's base for air attacks against Calcutta—for, with this defeat, Japan's westward invasion tide started to recede.

Winston Churchill was largely responsible for Lord Louis Mountbatten's appointment, and you may rest assured that Churchill didn't ask the Quebec Conference to appoint him to that position because he is rich, handsome, a great-grandson of Queen Victoria, and third cousin to the King of England. When Churchill urges the appointment of a man to a high military position, he doesn't care whether he spent much of his boyhood in a palace, as Lord Louis Mountbatten did, or whether he spent it shooting rabbits and trapping skunks in Kansas, as Eisenhower did.

Now it is true that Lord Mountbatten didn't win many battles early in the war. He didn't have half a chance to win most of the scraps he was in. But he has fought magnificently in the face of disastrous odds. Ships which he commanded have been bombed days on end; on two different occasions he had a destroyer blown out from under him. Dickie Mountbatten is sometimes called the most bombed officer in the British Navy, but nobody has ever questioned the aggressive fighting ability or the blazing courage of this dashing commander of royal blood.

The British say Lord Louis Mountbatten has "the Nelson touch." They compare him to the immortal hero of the battle of Trafalgar, Lord Horatio Nelson, that unsinkable old salt with one arm and with one eye who has become almost a patron saint to the men of the British Navy. Let me give you an illustration of how Lord Mountbatten, as commander of the British destroyer *Kelley,* demonstrated "the Nelson touch."

First, he brought the *Kelley* into port after she had been damaged by a mine. Then six months later, when the *Kelley* was repaired, Lord Mountbatten took her to sea again. This time she was hit by a torpedo which ripped open her forward boiler room. For four days and nights, Lord Mountbatten fought to get the *Kelley* back to port. He fought against the attacks of German torpedo boats, submarines, and bombers dropping explosives all around her. Finally a terrific storm blew up, and the waves of the North Sea smashed over her deck. She was completely disabled now and had to be towed by another destroyer. She might sink at any moment. Lord Mountbatten ordered all the men transferred to another destroyer—all except a few volunteers who remained aboard with him to keep the *Kelley's* guns blazing at the German bombers that were still

81

trying to sink her. Lord Mountbatten finally got the *Kelley* to a drydock and had her repaired.

A year later he took her into the battle again, and again demonstrated "the Nelson touch." That happened just after the Germans had conquered Greece and had seized the island of Crete by the use of paratroops. Those were dark and discouraging days for the British. The Germans ruled the air; but all was not lost, for Britannia still ruled the waves.

Lord Louis Mountbatten was in that fight up to his neck. He commanded the Fifth Destroyer Flotilla. Standing on the destroyer *Kelley,* Lord Mountbatten rushed in close to shore and shelled the German key positions on land. His destroyers sank a transport heavily laden with German troops and blew up an ammunition ship. For hours, German bombers tried to sink Lord Mountbatten's ship; hundreds of bombs were dropped, but every one missed. Shortly after eight o'clock, disaster struck! Dive-bombers screamed down out of the clouds, sending a bomb into the heart of the *Kelley.* Then down screamed another wave of deadly dive-bombers. Lord Mountbatten's ship was mortally wounded. In forty more seconds she would sink beneath the waves. But Mountbatten had "the Nelson touch"; he was determined that the *Kelley* would go down with every gun blazing. He yelled down the speaking tube to his men, "Whatever happens, keep the guns firing!" Forty seconds later the wounded ship turned turtle and sank. As she went down, Lord Mountbatten was washed off the bridge and plunged several feet beneath the water; then suddenly shot up to the surface again. As he reached the surface, he saw the propeller of his dying ship passing over his head and still racing at full speed in the air. For two and a half hours Lord Mountbatten and his men struggled in the sea, their eyes covered with a film of oil. They swam for hours while German bombers flew a few feet above them spraying them with machine-gun bullets;

but they were miraculously picked up later by one of their own destroyers. Yes, while battling German dive-bombers off the island of Crete, Lord Louis Mountbatten demonstrated "the Nelson touch."

Noel Coward's superb motion picture *In Which We Serve* was based largely on this experience of Lord Mountbatten..

Mountbatten first became known in America when he was named leader of the Commandos, that group of guerilla fighters that almost nightly raided the coasts of France, Belgium, and Holland. In each raid they harried the Germans, blew up military installations, wrecked enemy morale, boosted British spirits, and gathered valuable information about how to invade the Continent.

When Lord Mountbatten became head of the Commandos, he declared that he would never ask his men to do anything that he wouldn't do himself. He took part in Commando raids in which he and his men killed Germans with brass knuckles, leg spikes, daggers, clubs, blackjacks, and the long Commando knife.

Not only did Lord Louis take part in the Commando raids himself, but he also underwent the Commando training, the toughest training soldiers ever got in this or any other war. He himself led his men over the blood-and-sweat course which is part of the training of every Commando. First, while carrying a full pack and a rifle with bayonet fixed, he crawled through ten feet of badly tangled barbed wire. On he went, down a ravine, with bombs and mines exploding in every direction. Then he plunged through a ditch with water up to his neck, and through a wall of fire; then over a ten-foot barricade, with a wild charge uphill to the finish line. During all this, speakers were broadcasting German horror films, sound-track films made to strike terror into men's hearts, films filled with the sounds of explosions and dive-bombers and inhuman shrieks.

This is the kind of training that Mountbatten forced himself to go through as commander of the Commandos. He demonstrated that he had what it takes.

Lord Mountbatten is one of the youngest of our top-flight Allied leaders. He is forty-three—ten years younger than Eisenhower, twenty-one years younger than MacArthur. Yet as chief of combined operations he had to help work out one of the biggest planning jobs the world has ever seen—the landing in North Africa. He also helped plan the landings in Sicily and on the Italian mainland.

Lord Louis Mountbatten has spent more than two-thirds of his life in the British Navy. He entered the Navy when he was thirteen. That was inevitable; the call of the Navy was in his blood. Even as a child he played with toy battleships and dreamed of following in his father's footsteps. His father, the Marquis of Milford-Haven, served the British Navy for more than half a century and finally became First Lord of the Admiralty, the highest position in the British Navy.

Lord Mountbatten resolved years ago that he, too, would rise to a high place in the British Navy, just as his father had done. He knew that neither pull nor his royal blood would help. He knew that the only way to get to the head of the British Navy was by sheer merit and ability. He prepared himself the hard way. He studied so hard that he stood at the top in all his promotion and specialist examinations. He spent four years at Cambridge, getting a degree in electrical engineering. He did pioneer work in radio signaling and taught radio at the naval signal school for two years. He invented a number of devices now used in the British Navy.

Lord Mountbatten is said to have originated the well-known expression used in all the British fighting forces, "all tickey doo," meaning that everything is in perfect order.

Before Dickie Mountbatten undertakes any military mission, he insists on having everything "all tickey doo." When he was chief of the British Commandos, he always held a post-mortem examination after every raid. He was determined to find out what mistakes had been made so that the same mistakes would never be repeated. One day, after a raid on a Norwegian port, he called his men together for a conference and said, "Our timing went adrift somewhere. We were due to land at 8:30, but the first man didn't get ashore until 8:31." Was he joking? No, sir. He knew that lost seconds might mean lost lives. He was disturbed because the raid hadn't been "all tickey doo.'

Lord Louis· Francis Albert Victor Nicholas Mountbatten never starts a really big drive until he has everything "all tickey doo." And when he does start, he never stops. He has "the Nelson touch."

ONCE HE COULDN'T HOLD A JOB IN A STORAGE WAREHOUSE; BUT HE NOW HOLDS DOWN THE JOB OF BEING AMERICA'S FAVORITE COMEDIAN

THE ONLY MAN I KNOW OF who ever traveled eighty thousand miles for a laugh is Bing Crosby's next-door neighbor, Bob Hope. Eighty thousand miles—or more than three times the distance around the Equator—that's what Bob Hope covered to bring a smile to American boys in the service.

He's been bombed in Algiers. He got caught between an airport and an ammunition dump in Italy, when both were being shelled. And he's jounced around in trucks, tanks, and jeeps to crack jokes and rattle off his machine-gun humor wherever American troops have been longing for home.

At one place in England, Hope found out that six hundred men had tramped ten miles across the moors to catch his open-air show, then had started back, disappointed, when they couldn't get near. Without waiting for the last round of applause to die down, Hope piled his whole company into jeeps, went bounding off in pursuit of the soldiers, and ran through his entire routine again for their benefit, right there on the moors, in a drenching English rain.

No other performer on the American stage can equal Bob Hope's record. He was the first of all our entertainers to rush humor to the front lines, as a necessity of war. And he has not only played all over the European theater, but in every United States training camp—even Alaska.

86

Bob Hope

Up there in Alaska, Lieutenant-General Simon B. Buckner is in charge of operations, and one day Buckner got a very strange wire. "We sing, dance, and tell stories," the telegram informed him. "Have tuxedos and will travel. Can we play your circuit?" It was signed "Bob Hope."

When the answer came: "Yes!" Hope whirled his company up through Alaska and worked just as hard to bring down the rafters in those outposts and barracks as though he were heading the bill at the Palace back in New York. He even whistled up a gale of laughter the whole length and breadth of the Aleutian Islands, in tin huts and shanties, where men never get leave.

Bob Hope has been called the most thoroughly American of all our comedians, yet he's English by birth. His parents brought him over here to Cleveland before he'd cut his second molar, and by the time he was seven, he'd already decided he belonged to the stage.

It seems the local church gave a strawberry festival. Little Bob, who was still known as Leslie, got up to recite a poem. The first thing he knew, he'd balled up the lines, mispronounced all the words, and put his audience in stitches. Most kids of that age would have fled in disgrace; but Bob brightened up, cut a caper, and bowed—and discovered that the most wonderful kick he'd ever get out of life was to make people howl.

Twelve years later he was still so smitten with the lure of the stage that he couldn't forget it, even at work. Ostensibly, he had a job at night in an automobile warehouse, but when he found a dictaphone machine in the manager's office, he couldn't resist. He got the boys together, made up a quartet, and from then on they spent most of their nights cutting barbershop harmony on to dictaphone cylinders. Life was just one Sweet Adeline after another—till one morning the boss came into his office, turned on the machine, and was greeted by "There'll Be a Hot Time in the Old Town Tonight," off the record. Well,

off the record, there was a hot time in the old town that night—
and Leslie Townes Hope was out of a job.

He thought the thing over, decided he might as well be broke
as the way he was, and took to the stage. His act was with a
partner, singing and dancing, and for the next few years he ate
so many baked beans and doughnuts that even today his stomach
does a Highland Fling at the thought.

When the turning-point came, it was really by a fluke. The
manager of a little theater where he was playing asked him to go
out front and announce an act that was coming next week.
Bob said to the crowd: "Folks, the management wants me to
assure you that next week a *good* act is coming, and it's
called ——" They didn't let him finish. They whistled and
stamped, and for ten minutes straight he kept kidding himself
while they rolled in the aisles. When at last he walked off, the
manager said, "Bob, you're wasting your talents on singing and
dancing. You ought to do monologue." Bob took the hint,
struck out on his own, and he's been falling uphill all the way
ever since.

Four hundred thousand a year is what he makes now—and
out in Hollywood they say he knows how to keep it. A few years
back, an investment broker in Hollywood went to see the president of the bank in which Bob Hope has his largest account.
"Why don't you recommend me to Hope?" the broker requested. "As his business manager, I could give him a lot of
useful advice." "Oh, yes?" said the banker, "I've been watching
Bob Hope for the last three years—and you'd be better off if
he handled your money!"

There's only one main chance this quick young man with the
ski-slide nose ever let slip past him. That was when, in 1930,
he was asked to go into radio. "Sorry," Bob sniffed, "but I
can't waste my time. Radio will never get to first base."

Five years later, when radio was up in the major leagues, Bob
got a second opportunity. By now he was so eager to make good

on the air waves that he stayed up all night preparing his script. But when he reached the studios, he found he was supposed to go on without any audience, and, as Hope says, nothing gives him stage-fright like an empty seat.

Next door, he discovered, Charlie McCarthy and Edgar Bergen were in the midst of a broadcast and the studio was jammed. So Bob bribed an usher, strung up some velvet guide ropes leading from Bergen's studio to his, and then, when the crowds filed out, he cried: "This way, folks—this way to the exit!" The bewildered throngs milled into the studio, and he gave his first radio performance to a mob he'd shanghaied.

Bob Hope, in real life, is so crackling with energy and pep he hates to sit down. He does so many things at once that someone once described him as "the perfect portrait of a man in a hurry." As a matter of fact, he even has a special cord put on his telephone; it is several yards long, so he can walk around the room while he talks. He rarely stays still long enough to browse through a book, but he loves to read the funnies.

Those gags he rips off with such sparkling spontaneity are the careful result of labor and sweat. His most precious possession is a huge file of jokes, which he houses in a stoutly-bolted chamber adjoining his bedroom—and no one but himself ever handles the key. In addition to that, six gag writers beat out their brains for him all the year round, polishing every quip and quirk with the love and skill that Tiffany gives to diamonds.

One hundred and thirty million Americans hold their sides at his mirth, and about the only one who doesn't is Dolores, his wife. She thinks he's funny on the screen, she enjoys him in radio, but he can never get so much as a chuckle in the house. "I don't know what's wrong with me," Mrs. Hope says, "but when Bob wise-cracks at home, it just lays an egg!"

Like a good many actors, Hope is superstitious. When Paramount Studios offered to build a new dressing room for him, he refused to give up the one he had used when he made his first picture. That was so small and cramped it was almost a cupboard. Now Paramount has an elaborate suite of rooms *around* that cubbyhole, and Bob Hope can make up in front of his original mirror without inviting a hoodoo or risking a jinx.

Some day he hopes he may win an Oscar—one of those bronze statuettes Hollywood awards for outstanding performances. "Frozen Quiz Kids," he calls them. But Oscar or not, Bob Hope won first place in the hearts of our troops at the front, and he brings countless hours of fun to Americans at home. That, I think, is doing pretty well for a young man who says: "I've only been serious about one thing in life. And that is—a laugh!"

HE IS A HERO OF TWO WARS, YET HE WAS ONCE TOO SHY TO SAY "GOOD MORNING"

CAPTAIN EDDIE RICKENBACKER, President and General Manager of the Eastern Air Lines, has lived a life crowded with fiery drama and thrilling, hair-raising adventures.

As one of America's most famous racing drivers, Eddie Rickenbacker has faced death in racing cars that hurtled through the air end over end; and as America's most famous ace during World War I he faced death in air battles. He was almost killed in an airplane crash near Atlanta in 1941; and despite injuries so serious that for many weeks he was not expected to live, he personally directed the rescue workers who came to aid him and his flying companions. You will remember that he almost died of hunger and thirst and exposure when his plane crashed into the Pacific Ocean in 1942 and he and his six companions drifted about on rubber rafts hopelessly lost for three weeks.

Here is the strange part of the story. Eddie Rickenbacker said to me, when I interviewed him: "No one should fear death. I know, because I have come face to face with death several times. It is really a pleasant experience. You seem to hear beautiful music and everything is mellow and sweet and serene —no struggle, no terror, just calmness and beauty. When death comes, you will find it to be one of the easiest and most blissful experiences you have ever had."

Today Eddie Rickenbacker is one of the bravest and most

91

courageous men on this earth; yet as a boy he was so timid, so shy and self-conscious, that he would cross the street to avoid saying "good morning" to the neighbors. He knew that if he wanted to achieve happiness and success in life, he must conquer this shyness, so he forced himself to act brave. He joined the neighborhood gang and he put so much enthusiasm into the gang and gave them so many ideas that he soon became their leader.

Then sudden tragedy struck. His father was killed instantly in a bridge building accident. Little Eddie Rickenbacker quit school at once and became the chief bread winner for the family of seven. His first job was working in a glass factory on the night shift—twelve hours a night at five cents an hour.

He walked seven miles to the factory each night, and he walked seven miles home again in the morning—a total of fourteen miles a day—to save ten cents carfare which he gave to his mother.

He worked in the glass factory, then a shoe factory, then in the machine shops of the Pennsylvania Railroad at Columbus, Ohio. But he hated all these jobs. He was dreadfully unhappy because he longed to be an artist, a painter. He studied art in night school. Then one day a monument dealer tried to sell his mother a headstone to be erected over the grave of Eddie's father.

As the monument dealer talked, Eddie Rickenbacker's heart beat high with excitement. Here was opportunity—a Heaven-sent opportunity. Why not get a job chiseling angels on tombstones? In that way he could learn to be a sculptor while he was making a living. So with a sweep of enthusiasm, Eddie persuaded the tombstone dealer to hire him—and Eddie chiseled the inscription on the headstone that now stands above his father's grave.

At the end of the year Eddie Rickenbacker had to give up his work as a tombstone artist because the dust from the stone was getting into his lungs. His mother feared he was going to die from tuberculosis.

Then one day when he was fourteen years old, an event happened that changed Eddie Rickenbacker's entire life. One morning he saw a horseless carriage go chugging down a street in Columbus, Ohio—a one-cylinder Orient Buckboard car, sputtering and coughing along at about ten miles an hour. "I ran down the street after the car," Eddie Rickenbacker said, as he told me the story. "I was terribly excited. I was so excited about automobiles that I got a job in the first garage that opened up in town. It was merely a wooden barn that housed the first three cars that were bought in Columbus. While the boss was out, I learned to drive the cars."

Yes, Eddie Rickenbacker was so excited about automobiles that he decided to make one himself. He couldn't afford to buy tools, so he made his own tools and built his own workshop in the backyard. Within a few months, he had built an engine that actually ran. He had practically completed the chassis when suddenly a small automobile factory opened up in Columbus.

Eddie Rickenbacker was determined to get a job in that factory. He was so determined that he went to the factory every Sunday morning for eight months and applied for a job—and he was turned down every Sunday for eight months. He was only fourteen. The factory needed mechanics, not boys. The average boy would have been discouraged, but Eddie Rickenbacker wasn't. He was so determined to work there that he walked into the factory early one morning and, without saying a word to anyone, he picked up a broom and began sweeping the steel shavings off the floor and cleaning the benches around the machines.

The boss was astonished. "I'm going to work here," Eddie Rickenbacker said, "regardless of whether you pay me or not."

Talk about initiative and enthusiasm and determination! Eddie Rickenbacker knew what he wanted and he went after it like a bulldog. The boss hired him to do odd jobs around the factory at a dollar a day. One day as the boss walked through the factory at noon, he saw something that surprised and delighted him. The factory workers had eaten their lunches and were smoking, playing cards, and telling stories; but there over in the corner all by himself, the boss saw Eddie Rickenbacker, studying a correspondence course in mechanical engineering. The boss was impressed; two weeks later he put the fourteen-year-old boy in the engineering department of the factory and raised his salary.

Rickenbacker said to me: "I hadn't even finished the seventh grade in school, and if I hadn't studied that correspondence course in mechanical engineering, if I hadn't spent my spare time trying to improve myself, I would never have gotten anywhere."

From that time on his rise was rapid: workman, foreman, assistant engineer, trouble man, salesman, branch manager.

Then the lust for speed, the craving for adventure, got into his blood. The glamour and excitement of racing captured his heart. By the time he was twenty-five, Eddie Rickenbacker was one of the most famous racing-drivers in America.

When we entered the first World War in 1917, Eddie Rickenbacker was the idol of the automobile world; he sailed for France as General Pershing's staff-driver. But driving a General about behind the lines was too tame for his adventurous blood. He craved action, and he got it. After only five weeks of air training, he was given wings, and within a few months he had twenty-six victories to his credit and had written his name at the very top of the list of America's War Heroes.

When he landed in New York after the war, a great banquet was given in his honor by the automobile industry. His home town of Columbus, Ohio, wanted to present him with a huge home built by public subscription; and half a million people applauded and screamed with excitement as he was pulled through the streets of Los Angeles in an automobile florally decorated as an airplane.

But the most astonishing thing that Eddie Rickenbacker told me was his experience with Herman Goering in Germany, after the first World War. Eddie Rickenbacker and his bride were on their honeymoon touring Europe. As soon as they reached Berlin, four of the most famous aviators in Germany called to pay their respects. Back in 1918 these aviators had tried to kill one another in air battles; but all that had happened four years previously and soldiers don't hold grudges, so these German airmen called on Eddie Rickenbacker at the Hotel Adlon in Berlin and greeted him like a long-lost friend.

One of these men was Herman Goering, the man who was to build and command Hitler's air force. Goering said to Eddie Rickenbacker (remember, this was only four years after Germany had been conquered): "Germany's whole future is in the air and we are going to recapture the German Empire by air power. We are going to do three things," Goering continued. "First, we will teach gliding as a sport to all the young men in Germany. No one will object to that. Then we will build up commercial aviation. Then, after several years, when the democracies are sick of war, we will create a skeleton of a military air force—very small at first. Then we will put all these three together and keep on building, and then, while France and England are sleeping and unprepared, we will strike and win the next war."

Mind you, Goering said that at a time when Germany was weak and helpless. Goering said that years before Hitler had ever been heard of outside of his little gang. Goering said that while Germany was lying helpless in the throes of inflation and financial chaos, a bum among nations.

In 1943 Eddie Rickenbacker issued a warning of seventy-seven words—a warning that ought to be cast in bronze and hung in every home and every school in America, and in the halls of Congress: "Unless we keep a skeleton of our Allied armies in Germany and Japan until this generation of fanatics dies out and until a new generation learns the true meaning of democracy, unless we keep the Germans and the Japs from manufacturing even one plane, one tank, or one submarine—unless we do this, Germany and Japan will rearm again and attack us again, and our boys will again be dying on the battlefields of Europe and Asia."

HE EARNED FIVE THOUSAND DOLLARS A DAY, YET HE SEARCHED GARBAGE CANS FOR FOOD FOR HIS PET VULTURE

ONE HOT SUMMER DAY in 1876 a young Englishman dropped in to the old Hoffman House Bar in New York and ordered a whisky and soda *without ice*. The customers at the bar were astonished to hear anyone order a drink without ice on that hot day, and they were amused at his silk hat, his monocle, and his precise Oxford accent. A gay young blade at the bar acted as a self-appointed committee of one to ridicule the English dude. Putting a silver dollar in his eye, the rich New York socialite and athlete leaned over and said: "I say, Percy, I suppose Scotch and soda without ice is the English way, wot?"

He didn't know then that this silk-hatted chap had been the amateur lightweight boxing champion of England during his student days at Oxford. He didn't know it, but he was going to acquire the information with dramatic suddenness, for the Englishman removed his monocle carefully, pressed his silk hat more firmly on his head, and then, with extreme politeness, answered, "I beg your pardon, sir, but allow me to show you the English way." And he drove a swift haymaker to the New Yorker's jaw. When the gay blade regained consciousness, five minutes later, he shook hands with the English dude who had knocked him out and ordered drinks for everybody—drinks without ice! The crowd cheered.

This silk-hatted Englishman who packed dynamite in his

97

punch bore a name that was destined to make American theatrical history, a name that was destined to sparkle in electric lights for years, above thousands of theaters on five continents. His name was Barrymore, Maurice Barrymore, father of the fabulous Ethel, Lionel, and John Barrymore.

The Barrymores became the most famous theatrical family of the twentieth century. They were not only famous stars on the Broadway stage, but Lionel and John became two of the most celebrated stars in Hollywood. The Barrymores were so famous that *The Royal Family,* a play about them and their relatives, was the hit of Broadway seventeen years ago.

Strangely enough, none of the Barrymore children wanted to be actors. The two boys longed to be artists. Lionel disliked acting so thoroughly that he was delighted when his Grandmother Drew fired him from her production of *The Rivals,* because now he could do the thing he really wanted to do: become an artist and paint theatrical scenery.

Lionel studied art for a while in Paris, and John got a job drawing illustrations and cartoons for Arthur Brisbane, editor of the New York *Journal.* One of his weekly assignments was to illustrate Ella Wheeler Wilcox's "Poems of Passion." John paid no attention whatever to what these poems said; he merely drew whatever amused him. For example, he once illustrated one of Mrs. Wilcox's fiery love sonnets with a drawing of a dead man hanging by a rope from the limb of a tree. Mrs. Wilcox took her literary career very seriously. She was indignant. Flying into a rage, she demanded to see the artist who was ridiculing her poetry. When the young, handsome Barrymore called at her home, the middle-aged poetess was delighted and thrilled. She invited him to tea and insisted that hereafter the charming John Barrymore must always illustrate her poems.

Three weeks later, Brisbane fired the charming John for incompetence and negligence!

I once asked Lionel Barrymore if he and John were ever

broke and hungry while trying to make the grade as artists. "Yes," he replied, "lots of times, because we couldn't sell our sketches to the magazines. Of course, we could always get money by wiring home, but sometimes we didn't have enough money to send a wire. Jack and I spent the winter of our discontent in a bare studio on 14th Street," he continued, "but we didn't have any money to buy furniture. In fact we didn't even have a bed. We slept on the floor. We didn't have any blankets, so we slept in our overcoats with newspapers tucked inside them. Sometimes we even piled books on top of us to keep warm. There was another chap, Frank Butler, a writer, living with us, and he had a removable gold tooth. When we were broke, we pawned his tooth. I remember we tried every pawnshop on the East Side, but we could never raise more than seventy cents on that tooth."

One day John Barrymore and Butler were hungry. They had pawned the tooth, but had partaken of a little entertainment and had only ten cents of their treasure left. They went to a cheap lunchroom where you could get hot cakes and two cups of coffee for ten cents. John waited outside impatiently until Butler had ordered the second cup of coffee and had eaten half the hot cakes. Then Barrymore dashed in and whispered in Butler's ear and Butler jumped up and moaned, "Oh! No! It can't be true! My poor mother!" He then dashed out of the lunchroom, while Jack sat down and drank the second cup of coffee and finished the hot cakes.

Lionel and Jack Barrymore were cold and hungry in those days, but they were touched by the stuff that dreams are made on. Lionel now looks back on those days with nostalgic memories. He recently composed an orchestral suite in memory of John and the days of their youth. It was played for the first time April 22, 1944, by the Philadelphia Symphony Orchestra, under the direction of Eugene Ormandy. This composition is gay in spots with the lilt of gypsy melodies and folk songs that the brothers Barrymore used to hear in a Second Avenue cafe when the adventure of life seemed bright and endless. Lionel declared that writing this composition seemed like having a long visit with Jack.

Lionel Barrymore told me that his father's hobby was collecting animals. His father used to ship home bears, monkeys, wildcats, and a wide assortment of dogs. John and Lionel spent one summer in a farmhouse on Staten Island with no one for company but an old Negro servant and thirty-five dogs of all shapes, sizes, breeds, and colors.

Neither Lionel nor John ever lost his love of animals. A cat once had kittens in the space between the walls of Lionel's house in Hollywood, and he had a bit of the wall torn out for fear the kittens might die in that small space.

John had a pet monkey that he named Clementine. He cared for this monkey as if it were a child, took it on cruises with him, and let it eat at the same table with him.

He paid nineteen hundred dollars for two birds of paradise and spent twenty thousand dollars building an enormous aviary with a special heating apparatus to keep the air warm for his large collection of delicate tropical birds.

He once bought a huge king-vulture and made a pet of it. This vulture was as large as a goose and had a long, wicked beak. Like all vultures, it had a fondness for tainted meat. Occasionally John Barrymore, the romantic actor who drew a salary of five thousand dollars a day, would poke around Hollywood garbage cans to get the right kind of meat for his vulture. One night Barrymore, dressed in shabby working clothes, was walking along the street inspecting garbage cans. A well-dressed man saw him and mistook him for a hungry man searching in garbage cans for food for himself. The generous stranger gave Barrymore a quarter. "Be sure you spend it only for food," he advised. Barrymore touched his shabby hat humbly and murmured, "God bless you, sir!"

John Barrymore made over three million dollars in Holly-

John Barrymore

wood. He made almost half a million in one year alone, the year 1931. He paid a quarter of a million for a house and almost a quarter of a million dollars for a yacht. He spent eight thousand dollars to erect a shaft with a sundial in his swimming pool. He bought a chandelier that had once hung in the palace of the Archduke Francis Ferdinand, whose assassination touched off the first World War. Barrymore paid only seventy-five dollars for the chandelier, but he spent three thousand dollars to build a room to hang it in.

In 1934 he went to India for his health. He made about 75,000 dollars that year and spent almost 300,000 dollars—four times as much as he made. The next year it was much worse. During five months of 1935, he spent at the rate of 825 dollars a day, while his income was thirty-three dollars a day. His spending was then twenty-five times as much as his income, but he was spending mostly on other people.

His intimate friend Gene Fowler says that "Barrymore cared not at all for clothes. He didn't own a watch. He wore no rings. He entertained infrequently. He much preferred to eat a herring in the kitchen, or if possible in some friend's kitchen, to sitting in costly fashion at a restaurant table. He seldom had much pocket money. Aside from his almost fierce desire to see that all his bills be paid, he did not appear to bother much about money."

Jack Barrymore had friends among the lowliest and the highest. One of his friends was a hobo; another was Winston Churchill. It was Winston Churchill's encouragement that persuaded John Barrymore to continue his run of *Hamlet* in London after he had decided to close it.

Barrymore clowned through life with little regard for conventions. One night while playing Hamlet, he wanted to show off a bit; so between the acts he went out before the curtain dressed as Hamlet, in tights, and while a musician played a saxophone, Jack did a tap dance, a cake walk, and a waltz.

Another night, while playing a love scene in the romantic

101

Peter Ibbetson, he kissed a bouquet of flowers and pressed them to his heart. A young girl in the second balcony laughed. Barrymore lost his temper and shouted, "If you think you can play this scene better than I can, come down and do it!" As he said this, he flung the bouquet into the audience and struck a woman in the face. The curtain was rung down immediately. The theater was filled with angry denunciations. The manager feared there might be a riot. The play was halted for half an hour, and before the curtain rose again the manager warned the actors to run if trouble started. When Jack walked on the stage, there was silence at first; but he won the audience immediately by his poise, charm, and brilliant acting; and a minute later the audience broke suddenly into a prolonged cheer.

On another occasion, during a flu epidemic, Barrymore was irritated by the incessant coughing of the audience. He hid a big fish under his coat and when the audience began coughing he threw the fish over the footlights and yelled, "Busy yourselves with *this,* you blasted walruses!"

Once while John was speaking the famous lines in *Richard the Third:* "A horse, a horse! My kingdom for a horse," a man in the balcony laughed loudly. Barrymore immediately pointed his sword toward the balcony and shouted, "Make haste and saddle yonder braying ass!"

John Barrymore was unquestionably one of the outstanding Hamlets of our time. He played Hamlet on Broadway longer than any other actor. So it is altogether fitting that Lionel had carved on his brother's tomb the words, "Good Night, Sweet Prince"—words uttered by Horatio as Hamlet lay dying in his arms. "Good night, sweet Prince, and flights of angels sing thee to thy rest."

AT SIXTY HE ATTENDED BURLESQUE SHOWS; AT NINETY-THREE HE READ PLATO TO IMPROVE HIS MIND

I'M GOING TO TELL YOU about a man who has had a profound effect on the thinking of this nation, especially its legal thinking. He was one of the greatest intellectual giants this country has ever produced; yet he was so human he loved to run to fires, often attended burlesque shows, and was so fond of detective stories that he finally had to ration himself to one or two good, bloody murders a week!

That man was Justice Oliver Wendell Holmes. Born when this nation had only twenty-seven states, he died just nine years ago at the age of ninety-four.

Oliver Wendell Holmes had known most of the big men this nation produced in the last hundred years. As a youngster he had sat for hours discussing books with Ralph Waldo Emerson. And his own father, Dr. Oliver Wendell Holmes, was famous the world over as the Autocrat of the Breakfast Table—the man who had written "Old Ironsides" and "The One-Hoss Shay."

When Holmes was a boy, his father told the children that whoever got off the wittiest remark at the family table would get an extra heaping portion of marmalade or jam. And since Wendell liked marmalade, he quickly developed a very sharp tongue. This early training stayed with him all of his life. Seventy years later he couldn't resist making wise-cracks in the dignified sessions of the United States Supreme Court, and many of his remarks had to be stricken from the records!

He always said he didn't see why an intellectual had to be a stuffed shirt and not have any fun. One night in Washington, when his hair was snow-white, he went to a burlesque show. The performance was—well, let us say a bit snappy, and the Judge's thundering laughter could be heard for ten rows. All of a sudden he turned to a man sitting next him—an absolute stranger—and said, "I always thank God I'm a man of low tastes!" (And *that,* bear in mind, was the celebrated jurist whom England had just honored as the only man of law outside the British Empire ever to be made a member of the Honorable Society of Lincoln's Inn!) I suppose that never before in our public life have we had a figure who was such an astonishing combination of intellectual titan and plain common man.

When he began to study law, back in 1857, his father was horrified, for lawyers in those days were almost despised. "Don't do it, Wendy," the old man pleaded, "no one who takes up law can ever be great."

But Wendell had a notion that a man who studied law could *make* his life great, and he tore through Blackstone as though it were a novel with a thrill on every page.

By 1861 he was ready to graduate from Harvard; but when the Civil War came, he tossed his law books in the closet and marched off as a private, all dressed up in the baggy pantaloons, the sky-blue tunic, and the bright red cap of the Yankee Zouaves. Not the kind of outfit we'd think of today as being fit for a soldier, but Oliver Wendell Holmes could fight, all the same. He was wounded three times and once a bullet came so close to his heart that an Army doctor, passing by his stretcher, remarked, "No use to waste time even looking at that man— he's already dead!"

Dead? Why, as a matter of fact, that Boston Yankee hadn't even stopped growing! He was still an inch or two short of his six-feet-three, and he still had to render the first truly outstanding service he ever did for his country—for in 1864 he may have saved Lincoln's life!

Justice Oliver Wendell Holmes

While Grant was busy at Richmond, a band of Confederate raiders led by Jubal Early pushed their way up north and got as far as Alexandria, Virginia—only twenty miles from Washington.

There, at Fort Stevens, the Federal forces got ready to stop them. Abraham Lincoln, who'd never seen a battle, hurried down to the Fort. He was actually standing on the roof near one of the parapets when the firing first opened. His tall, lanky figure, unmistakable to everyone, was in plain view of the enemy guns.

One of the generals spoke up and said, "Don't you think, Mr. President, you'd better step back?" But Lincoln paid no attention. Five feet away, a man thrust his head above the edge of the parapet and reeled back, dead. Three feet away, another man fell.

Suddenly, just behind Lincoln, a voice yelled out, "Get down, you fool! Get out of line!" Lincoln swung around, to face young Captain Holmes, who was glaring at him fiercely, with fire in his eyes. "Well, Captain," Lincoln smiled, "I see you know how to speak to civilians!" Nodding approval, Lincoln stepped out of range.

Naturally, when that story got around, Oliver Wendell Holmes was hailed as a hero, but he squelched it all quickly. "Don't call me a hero," he snapped. "I trust I did my duty as a soldier respectably, but nothing I did was remarkable at all."

Nothing remarkable? Well, after all, perhaps what was more remarkable about this young man was that when the war was over he brushed off his hands as though nothing had happened, and went back to school. He knew he wasn't apt to make very much money when he mastered the law, for there was a saying in those days: "If a lawyer pays for his sign the first year, he's doing very nicely."

Oliver Wendell Holmes didn't even make that much! In fact, he was thirty years old before he could pay for his own Boston beans. I mean that literally. When at the age of thirty he married Fannie Dixwell, his childhood sweetheart, neither of them had a cent of his own. They had to live in a third-floor bedroom in Dr. Holmes's house. And what's more, it took Fannie Holmes one solid year of scrimping and saving to get enough money to enable them to move. And even after they moved, their new home was just a couple of rooms above a drugstore; all they had to cook on was a one-ring gas flat.

Yes, there he was, the son of a genius, and at thirty years old he had not even started.

To help fill up his time, he began to re-edit and bring up to date a great legal classic, the *Commentaries of American Law*. The labor involved was stupendous. It meant studying and annotating thousands of cases, countless opinions handed down by the courts. As the years wore on, with the end of his task not even in sight, Holmes himself began to be worried. He believed that a man must make his mark before he is forty, and he was now thirty-nine.

"D'you think I'll make it, Fannie?" he used to ask his wife, looking up from his desk when the clock had struck midnight. And Fannie, with her sewing in her lap, would say, "You'll make it, Wendell. I *know* that you will!"

He did make it, too. For that book, which is now regarded as a towering milestone in American law, came off the presses exactly five days before his fortieth birthday, and he and his wife toasted the event with a pint of champagne.

Harvard University was so impressed that it offered him a professorship at 4500 dollars a year if he'd come and teach law. Would he teach law! He was dizzy with the honor, but being a shrewd Boston Yankee, he went to his friend, George Shattuck, and asked his advice.

"Grab at it, Wendell," Shattuck advised, "but insist on a clause. If you get a chance to be appointed a judge on the Massachusetts bench, you've the right to resign." Be appointed a judge! Holmes laughed out loud at the very idea. But all the same, he did as Shattuck told him.

Justice Oliver Wendell Holmes

And that was the luckiest thing he ever did in his life! For in less than three months, Shattuck came running to Harvard and dragged the Professor right out of a class. "Great news!" he gasped. "Otis Lord has resigned, leaving a vacancy in the Massachusetts Supreme Court. The Governor wants *you*—but he has to file your name with the Council before twelve o'clock. It is now eleven!"

Only one hour! Holmes grabbed his hat and the two of them almost raced through the streets to the Governor's mansion. One week later Oliver Wendell Holmes, with the title of Justice, took his place on the Supreme Court of Massachusetts. And that, he always said, was the one stroke of lightning that transformed his life. That was the turning point.

It was on the Massachusetts bench that Holmes first became known as the Great Dissenter, because he so often disagreed with the other judges. For example, in 1896 a case came up which questioned the right of labor to picket a shop. Holmes, who had never worked with his hands a day in his life, upheld that right. After he had handed in his decision, he remarked to a friend, "I have just shut myself off forever from judicial promotion." That's what he thought; but he did it all the same, for this man was never swayed one iota by personal interests. The only thing he cared for was what he believed was right.

Yet, strangely enough, that decision and others which he believed had ended his career, opened up the way for even greater advancement. For Teddy Roosevelt, in Washington, was busy just then fighting the Trusts, using his Big Stick to smash the monopolies. So when he heard about Holmes, he roared, "There's a judge! There's a man I want!"

And as fast as he could push through the appointment, Roosevelt placed Holmes in the Supreme Court of the United States—the greatest judicial honor this country can bestow. Roosevelt took it for granted that his new appointee would vote as he wanted. But he was wrong. On the first big case, Holmes decided against the President and Theodore Roosevelt was so

107

furious he yelled in disgust, "Why, I could carve out of a banana a judge with more backbone than that!"

Roosevelt was mad, but the people were delighted. Holmes was just what they wanted—a judge who didn't belong to anyone, a judge who belonged only to himself. During the next thirty years, Oliver Wendell Holmes went right on dissenting till he became a sort of national legend—the most respected man who ever sat on the Supreme Bench in this land.

One of the most colorful figures in Washington life, Holmes would never give interviews, for he hated publicity. Yet some things about his private life were bound to leak out. For instance, he and his wife were fond of animals. They not only kept a menagerie of birds, but they also had two monkeys and three flying squirrels which flew around their bedroom. Sometimes during the day the Judge would doze off in Court because he hadn't had enough sleep the night before—he had been awakened too often by the three flying squirrels landing like dive-bombers smack on his bed.

Up till the time he was well in his eighties, Holmes refused to take an elevator and bounded upstairs two steps at a time. Whenever a fire alarm sounded, he and his wife would dash out of the house and run to the fire. The language this cultured New Englander used when he wasn't in Court was more like a pirate's than a Boston Brahmin's. He always addressed his secretaries (men like Francis Biddle) as Sonny, Young Feller, and Idiot Boy.

In 1928 a Washington reporter asked a mechanic in overalls, "Does the name Oliver Wendell Holmes mean anything to you?"

The mechanic grinned. "Sure! He's the young judge in the Supreme Court who's always disagreeing with the old guys!" When Holmes heard that, he enjoyed a good laugh, for he was then eighty-seven—practically the oldest judge in the Court.

Holmes had always said, "I shall not resign till the Almighty

108

Justice Oliver Wendell Holmes

"Himself tells me to quit!" At the age of ninety-one his health began to fail. When he got down from the Bench, he had to be helped by two other judges. One day he said to the clerk, "I won't be in tomorrow. . . . I won't be in tomorrow"—and he never went back.

Two years later, when this grand old man reached his ninety-third birthday, Franklin Delano Roosevelt, who had just been sworn into office, came to pay his respects. He found Justice Holmes sitting in his study with a volume of Plato. Roosevelt inquired, "Tell me, Mr. Justice, why are you reading Plato?"

Holmes replied, "To improve my mind."

Think of it! Ninety-three! To improve his mind!

Yes, this country has never produced a man of finer character than Oliver Wendell Holmes, nor one who has had greater influence on our laws. His decisions will influence your life and mine for many years to come. And here is something else you might like to know, too:

When Justice Holmes died, he willed all his money—a quarter of a million dollars—to the United States Government. He gave all of his books to the Library of Congress, to be used by the people he had so brilliantly served.

109

ONE OF GREAT BRITAIN'S MOST FAMOUS LEADERS MARRIED A WOMAN WHO REFUSED TO HAVE CHILDREN UNDER THE BRITISH FLAG

WHOM WOULD YOU NAME as the five most important Allied leaders in World War II? We would probably all agree on the first four: Roosevelt, Churchill, Stalin, Chiang Kai-shek. But whom would you put fifth? My candidate for fifth place is Jan Smuts, Field Marshal. The Right Honorable Jan Christian Smuts, Prime Minister of South Africa—an empire one-sixth the size of the United States—is famous as a statesman, philosopher, scholar, soldier, scientist.

If it had not been for one speech made by Jan Christian Smuts, South Africa would probably have remained neutral in the war.

It was like this:

At the outbreak of the European war in 1939, the South African Parliament met to declare a qualified neutrality. James Hertzog was then Prime Minister of South Africa. He was violently opposed to joining England in another war against Germany. So were most of his followers. Many of them secretly wished—well, as a matter of fact, there was nothing secret about it; many of them openly and vociferously wanted— Hitler to win. Why? Because many of the Boers had never forgiven England for the Boer War fought back at the turn of the century. That was the war in which England conquered the

110

Jan Christian Smuts

descendants of the Dutch colonists who had settled South Africa eighty years before George Washington was born. Many of the Boers wanted to secede from the British Empire and form a republic of their own. A secret ballot had already been taken showing that the Parliament was overwhelmingly in favor of neutrality. Then Jan Smuts rose to speak. It was a momentous occasion, and he knew it. Jan Smuts knew that if Germany won the war, Hitler would rule South Africa with bayonets. He pleaded with the South African Parliament to declare war on Germany, not for England's sake, but for her own sake. Speaking with the impassioned fervor of a Patrick Henry, he won by the narrow margin of only thirteen votes.

Hitler is reported to have laughed when South Africa declared war—and why not? Its white population was less than Chicago's. It had no navy—not even one fighting ship. Its air force was inferior to Hollywood's. Its inadequately trained army numbered less than forty thousand. It had two tanks and an equal number of armored cars. It had enough shells for a one-day battle—provided it were not a very hard battle. It had just one small industry equipped to do war work.

Jan Smuts didn't dare to resort to conscription for the Army. Conscription might have meant civil war. So he pleaded for volunteers with such fervor that fifteen out of every hundred white males in South Africa flocked to the colors.

If the same proportion of our population had volunteered for army service, we would have had a volunteer army of thirteen million.

Jan Smuts remembered that during the first World War, civil war had broken out because South Africa was going to fight beside England. Jan Smuts fixed it this time so there couldn't be any civil war. He ordered all private citizens owning rifles to sell them to the Government or else pay an enormous fine. Seventy thousand hunting rifles were sold to the Government and the opposition thus peacefully disarmed.

111

When Hitler's armies swept over Poland, South Africa had just one war plant—a plant that made a million rifle shells a month. This production was stepped up to a million every day. Jan Smuts had a soft drink plant turned into a howitzer factory; he had a bridge factory converted into a plant making armored cars. A watch factory was switched to making bombs.

Few men now living have such a vast accumulation of knowledge as has Jan Smuts; yet up until he was twelve years of age, he could neither read nor write. As a child, he was sickly and afflicted with the rickets. His own father described him as "a poor, unhealthy youngster, a queer fellow without much intelligence." That was *his own father's* description of the boy who today has become a world-famous scholar and the most powerful figure in South Africa.

When he attended Victoria College in South Africa, Jan Smuts refused to live in a college dormitory. He felt he couldn't afford to waste time in idle chatter and recreation. In order to avoid that temptation, he boarded with a private family and, incidentally, married the girl who lived across the street from his boarding house. They have reared six children.

For two reasons Jan Smuts quickly distinguished himself in school. First, because he developed an insatiable thirst for knowledge. He read all the time. He didn't play any games, didn't associate with the other boys, just read, read, read—twelve to fifteen hours a day. Once he stayed up all night to master a difficult mathematics problem which *no one else* in the class was able to solve.

The second reason why Jan Smuts progressed so rapidly in school was because he had an astonishing memory. He rarely forgets anything he reads. When he is challenged to demonstrate his memory, he points to his library which consists of over ten thousand volumes, and says: "You can pick out any one of those ten thousand books, open it at any page you wish, read any paragraph on that page, and I'll tell you the substance

112

Jan Christian Smuts

of the paragraph following the one you read." Though many people have accepted that challenge, Jan Smuts has never yet failed to make good on his boast.

No wonder he knows forty times as much as you and I know! In college, he memorized a Greek grammar in six days. Sounds miraculous, and it is miraculous; but he did it. His astonishing memory enabled him to win a scholarship in Cambridge University, in England, and his memory made it possible for him to complete a two-year law course there in one year. Not only did he study twice as many subjects as anyone else in the Cambridge law school, but he stood at the head of both classes. Not a bad record for a young man whose father felt he didn't have much intelligence.

His performance at Cambridge was so brilliant that he was offered a professorship in Christ's College, as well as many other attractive positions in England; but he turned them all down and went back to South Africa to practice law.

However, Jan Smuts failed as a lawyer both in Capetown and in Johannesburg. He didn't know how to handle people. He was cold, domineering, always arguing, contradicting, and criticizing. He drove clients away and he antagonized judges and juries.

When the Boer War broke out in 1899, Jan Smuts demonstrated that he was an inspired military leader. In a few months this lawyer who had had no military training whatever was made a general. He led his band of Boer farmers for a thousand miles across South Africa, waging guerilla warfare, living off the country and the British. When the Boers needed rifles, ammunition, and horses, they raided the British camps and took them. Smuts started out with a ragged group of three hundred Boer farmers; but wherever he went, he attracted volunteers. When the war ended, his band of raiders had increased to ten times its original size.

Smuts achieved a sensational success in that campaign and

113

became a national hero. He deserved to be a hero because the entire Boer population of South Africa was then about the size of Cleveland, Ohio. Yet, these Boers, under the inspired leadership of men like Smuts, fought the British Empire—the richest and most powerful empire on earth—for three years before they were conquered.

While waging guerilla warfare against the British, Jan Smuts carried two books in his saddle bags. One was a copy of the New Testament, in Greek, and the other was Kant's *Critique of Pure Reason.*

Imagine a general, a few hours before he blows up a railroad bridge, reading the New Testament in Greek!

Imagine a general, after he has made a raid to capture ammunition and fresh horses, sitting before a campfire reading Immanuel Kant's *Critique of Pure Reason.*

Jan Smuts is not only Prime Minister of South Africa, he is the whole Government. He controls everything and everybody in South Africa—everybody, that is, except his wife! He and his wife sharply disagree about the English.

Jan Smuts was grateful to the English for giving the defeated Boers financial help and self-government at the close of the Boer War. Ever since, Jan Smuts has been one of Britain's most ardent allies.

But his wife has always been bitterly anti-British. Indeed, she vowed that none of her children would ever be born under the British flag. Since the British flag flew over all of South Africa, that took a bit of doing; but she did it. She did it by keeping a Boer Republic flag always unfurled over her bed.

"My husband warned me," she once said laughingly, "that I would probably be punished for my bitterness by our children marrying Englishmen."

Actually, two of her three daughters did marry Englishmen.

As Jan Smuts has grown older, he has lost some of his harshness and austerity; but, when working under a terrific strain, he occasionally loses his temper and flies into a rage. When-

114

ever he does, his wife doesn't go near him. She sends messages to him through his secretary.

His own children are impressed by his vast knowledge, power, and prestige; and they are always conscious of his cold, domineering manner. "My own children," General Smuts once said, "treat me like a distinguished stranger."

Jan Smuts refuses to live in the luxurious official residence of the Prime Minister of Africa. Instead, he lives on his own farm ten miles from the capital, in a house made of corrugated iron that he bought second-hand forty years ago for fifteen-hundred dollars. This iron house is crammed with stinkwood furniture, arrows, animal skins, an air-cooling unit, walking sticks, books, and old bits of railroad track.

Jan Smuts sleeps on the porch in an iron bed. He has a kitchen chair beside his bed on which is a cup of tea and a book, always a book. Field Marshal, the Right Honorable Jan Christian Smuts, Prime Minister of South Africa, always makes his own bed.

The landscaping around the Smuts home is quite in keeping with the building. There are no flowers in the yard, no well-kept lawn, no shrubs.

His grandchildren swing on an old automobile tire hanging from the limb of a tree and they play in a playhouse made out of old tin cans.

The hobbies of Prime Minister Smuts of South Africa are biology and botany. In an attempt to develop a strain of grass that will thrive on the dry hot stretches of the African veldt, he has grown fifty different kinds of grasses in one of his fields. He owns six thousand acres of land on which he has planted over half a million trees that will be cut someday and used for timber in the mines.

Jan Smuts signed the peace treaty that ended the first World War—signed it although every fiber of his being revolted against its injustices. If he has his way, we shall enjoy a long, just, and lasting peace.

A PHRENOLOGIST ADVISED HIS MOTHER— NOW HE ADVISES PRESIDENTS

TOWARD THE CLOSE of the last century a wild fight occurred on the baseball diamond at City College in New York. That fight affected the first World War, and it may affect your future. It was the ninth inning of a ball game; three men were on base. The batter hit a home run that won the game. At least the umpire ruled that the batter was safe at home. But the catcher was indignant. He swore there had been dirty work at the plate. He accused Bernard Baruch, the man who had hit the home run, of knocking him off the plate and making him drop the ball. Bernard Baruch hotly denied it. He told that catcher a thing or two. A fight broke out—a bloody fight. Baruch had been boxing for years; in fact, he was such a superb fighter that Bob Fitzsimmons, who later became heavyweight champion of the world, once suggested that he become a professional fighter. So that fight on the baseball grounds was duck soup for Barney Baruch. When the opposing players swung at him, he knocked them down right and left. One of the players that Baruch knocked down jumped up and grabbed a baseball bat. This player apparently had never heard of Queensbury rules—he hit Barney Baruch over the head with the baseball bat and knocked him out. The blow broke the drum in Baruch's left ear and made him almost deaf in one ear.

That broken eardrum changed Bernard Baruch's entire life. He had planned to go to West Point and become an officer in the regular Army. He got an appointment to West Point all right and he passed the entrance examinations. But West Point turned him down because his hearing was impaired. That broken eardrum forced Barney Baruch to forget all about a military career and go into business. He made millions in business and acquired a fabulous reputation. President Woodrow Wilson was so impressed by Baruch's business genius that he gave him the biggest business job that any man had ever had in American history. Woodrow Wilson gave him the job of running American industry during the first World War. Back in 1918 Bernard Baruch had the power to regulate or shut down practically any business. No manufacturer could get a pound of copper, iron, lumber, tin, or any other scarce commodity without his consent.

Woodrow Wilson took Bernard Baruch with him to Europe in 1919, as his economic advisor, to help write the peace treaty.

Bernard Baruch has tackled one of the toughest post-war problems—the problem of getting this nation out of war production and back into peace production without bankruptcies and vast, cruel unemployment.

Baruch's life was affected not only by a blow on the head with a baseball bat, but also by a visit to a phrenologist. His mother took him to the phrenologist, who claimed he could feel the bumps on a man's head and then tell what business or profession he ought to enter. He felt Bernard's head and said he ought to be a business man. Now Bernard Baruch wanted to be a surgeon like his father. He had his father's enthusiasm for medicine, and he studied medicine for a year. But his mother pleaded with him to go into business as the phrenologist advised. To please her, he got a job with a glassware concern at three dollars a week and studied law at night. Then his mother feared he might become a lawyer. Remembering what the phrenologist had advised, she kept saying to her son over and over: "Go where the money is, Barney. Go where the money is." He did.

117

Biographical Roundup

He went to Wall Street and played the stock market. About 99 per cent of all the speculators who play the stock market go broke. But Bernard Baruch made tens of millions in Wall Street—an astonishing record.

What was the secret of Bernard Baruch's astonishing success in Wall Street? Two things. First, he immediately won friends among the big shots in Wall Street. People were impressed by his charm, his contagious smile, his good looks, his gracious manners, his honesty, and his shrewdness. The big shots in the market took him to lunch; gave him advice, contacts, and opportunities. He quickly stepped up and up; and when he was only twenty-seven years old, Thomas Fortune Ryan paid Baruch 130,000 dollars for buying the Liggett & Meyers Tobacco Company.

The second and most important factor of Bernard Baruch's success in Wall Street was his passion for facts. When Baruch acts, there is always a reason—a reason based not on hearsay or wishful thinking, but on knowledge.

Bernard Baruch's ability to forecast the future by getting and studying and interpreting facts has made him one of the outstanding men of his generation. This ability made him the trusted advisor to five presidents: Wilson, Harding, Coolidge, Hoover, and Roosevelt. Woodrow Wilson nicknamed him "Doctor Facts."

Bernard Baruch once made a fortune in Wall Street almost by accident. The story goes like this: After months of research he concluded that there was a big overproduction of copper, that prices would fall, and that the 8-per-cent dividend on Amalgamated Copper would be cut. Therefore he sold Amalgamated Copper short by thousands of shares. The dividend was cut and the stock fell ten points in an hour. Bernard Baruch's associates wanted him to take a quick profit, but they were unable to reach him that day.

It was a religious holiday—the Day of Atonement. Bernard Baruch had promised his mother that he would spend that

118

Bernard Baruch

sacred day at home with her and have nothing to do with business. His associates were alarmed. If he bought back the stock immediately, he could make forty thousand dollars. If he waited until tomorrow, anything might happen. In desperation they kept his telephone ringing. They sent telegrams to his home. They sent messengers. They went in person. No use. Baruch couldn't be reached. He afterwards admitted that, if he had been at his office that day, he probably would have bought the stock back and made a quick profit of forty thousand dollars; since he couldn't act that day, he thought the matter over calmly the next day and decided to remain short of Amalgamated Copper. Within a year the stock dropped one hundred points and Baruch made a fortune on that deal alone.

He loved to make money and he loved to give it away. A few years ago he offered to give the United States Army three million dollars to buy machinery for making powder. He made the offer because he saw war coming and was alarmed at our unpreparedness.

During the last war he paid 85,000 dollars out of his own pocket to send a group of experts to Europe to get some facts the Government needed. This 85,000 dollars should have been paid by the Government because it was an expense item of the War Industries Board, but Baruch insisted on paying it himself.

In 1918 Baruch also insisted on building with his own money a hospital to care for victims of the terrible flu epidemic among the war workers in Washington.

When the War Industries Board disbanded at the close of the last war, Bernard Baruch paid fifty thousand dollars out of his own pocket to buy tickets to send stranded war workers back to their homes.

For years Bernard Baruch suffered from shyness and timidity because of a humiliating childhood experience. It was a bitter, cruel experience. He remembers it to this day. It taught him the tragedy of ridiculing children. It happened like this: At a party he and several other children were speaking memorized

119

Biographical Roundup

pieces before a group of adults. Bernard Baruch faced the audience and recited in sing-song fashion:

> On Linden, when the sun was low,
> All bloodless lay the untrodden snow;
> And dark as winter was the flow
> Of Iser, rolling rapidly.

One of the adults sitting in the front row began to mimic and ridicule little Bernie Baruch's manner of speaking. He was so hurt, so shocked, so humiliated that he fled from the room in tears and ran home filled with fear and discouragement.

That experience gave him a feeling of shyness that persisted for a lifetime. Even today Bernard Baruch refuses to speak in public unless he reads his talk.

Baruch discovered that one of the best ways to conquer shyness was to ignore it, to do the things he feared to do. One night when he was sixteen years old, he attended a coming-out party in a private home. He wore his father's dress suit; the suit was too large for him, so his mother had rigged it up with safety pins. When he arrived at the Fifth Avenue house where the party was being given, he was too shy and self-conscious to go upstairs and join in the festivities. Instead, he hid himself away in a room on a lower floor. Presently a man who was going to make a speech at the party came down to this lower floor and discovered Bernard Baruch hiding there in his ill-fitting dress suit. The would-be orator persuaded young Baruch to go upstairs with him. As soon as Baruch was introduced to a girl and started dancing—as soon as he got busy—his shyness vanished.

Bernard Baruch has a motto of seven words of advice from his father. These seven words have been the credo, the guiding star of his life. His father wrote them across the bottom of his photograph, and Bernard Baruch keeps this photograph on his bureau where he sees it every day. Here are the seven words:

"Always let unswerving integrity be your guide."

120

HOW A SHY, SELF-CONSCIOUS BOY BECAME
ONE OF AMERICA'S GREATEST
MILITARY LEADERS

ONE DAY A BOY SAT in a room on the banks of the Mississippi
River, near St. Louis, taking an examination. He had traveled
150 miles to take the examination, and now he feared he was
going to fail; he was terribly discouraged, for it was an examination to get into West Point. He wanted to go to West Point,
not because he was especially interested in a military career,
but because it was the only place he knew of where he could
get a college education free. And if he was going to get any
kind of a college education, it had to be free, because he had
no money. His father was dead and his mother was working as
a dressmaker and barely able to pay the grocery bill.

He got along fine in his examination until he came to
geometry; then he was stuck. He hadn't looked into a geometry
book for a long time. He tried hard to work the problems, but
he couldn't. He stopped. There was no use going on. He had
failed and he knew it.

He picked up his papers and started to go up to the officer
in charge and tell him he was quitting. But he noticed that the
officer was busy reading a newspaper; and the boy was so shy,
so self-conscious, that he couldn't get up the courage to disturb
the officer while he was reading. So while he was waiting for
the officer to stop reading, he began to study the geometry problems again—and a miracle happened. Slowly the facts that he
had once learned about geometry began to drift up from the

hidden depths of his mind. He passed the examination and entered West Point in 1911. That boy later became a professor of mathematics in West Point and one of the most brilliant field commanders in the American Army. His name is Bradley, Lieutenant-General Omar Nelson Bradley, and he directed the greatest United States striking force in World War II. He achieved victories with a speed that was beyond our wildest hopes when we first landed in France.

Omar Bradley may have been discouraged about his knowledge of geometry in 1911, but he graduated from West Point in 1915, forty-fourth place from the top of his class of 164. Ike Eisenhower lived right across the hall from Omar Bradley at West Point, and Eisenhower stood sixty-first from the top of that class, seventeen places lower than Omar Bradley. When it came to conduct, the shy Omar Bradley stood sixth place from the top of his class, while the gay, jovial Ike Eisenhower stood 125th from the top.

The West Point graduating class of 1915 is famous for producing more than thirty generals. Almost one man out of every five in that class has pinned on the stars of a general. And Omar Bradley was the first man in his class to become a general. The baseball team alone produced eight generals. Bradley, by the way, played left field on the baseball team and had a batting average of .383. He also played left tackle on the football team.

He is still interested in sports. His wife told me that he excels in all sports—especially in golf. He loves to fish and to hunt and he has a couple of bird dogs out in Missouri who can't understand why he never takes them out hunting any more.

His outdoor sports have kept him in splendid physical condition. In 1942, when he was forty-nine years old, he commanded the 28th Infantry Division during army maneuvers in Louisiana. In spite of his forty-nine years, he ran through obstacle courses and swung across ravines from dangling ropes while young men less than half his age fainted and fell from exhaustion.

Lieutenant-General Bradley

When General Bradley's daughter went away to college, he urged her to develop proficiency in sports. He knew that proficiency in sports would give her physical stamina, happiness, and popularity. His wife told me that he also taught their daughter to live by the golden rule. That is what General Bradley himself does, and that is why he has always been so popular with his men. He sometimes stands in line with the enlisted men and takes his turn at getting food. While he was teaching in the Infantry School at Fort Benning, Georgia, he often used to go out hunting and would frequently take an enlisted man with him as his companion.

Newsweek once said that General Bradley thinks of himself as an ordinary man. I asked his wife if that were true and she said, "Yes, definitely." He never puts on any swank, no side or fuss or feathers. The newspapers reported recently that he didn't even own a dress cap or a Sam Browne belt. I asked his wife if that report were correct and she said no, it wasn't. She said he owns a dress cap and a Sam Browne belt but he didn't take them overseas because, as he said, "I am going over there to fight, not to parade."

He is extremely modest and unpretentious. He was promoted to the temporary rank of Lieutenant-General in 1943. The newspapers carried the story. It was no secret. Everybody knew it, but Omar Bradley refused to pin the third star on his shoulder until the official orders were actually in his hands.

General Bradley is extremely polite and habitually speaks in a soft voice. He once declared that he had never known a strong man who found it necessary to raise his voice. But once in Sicily, General Bradley did raise his voice—but he didn't forget to say "please." It happened like this. He was interviewing a German officer who had just been captured, when suddenly one of his own aides accidentally fired off a gun. The bullet whizzed mighty close to Bradley's ear. He turned to his aide and said, "Be more careful with that damn thing—please."

123

Biographical Roundup

On another occasion, while watching men in bayonet practice, General Bradley shoved one of the men off balance to demonstrate the importance of keeping the right stance. After the demonstration, Bradley apologized to the man he had shoved. "I didn't mean to treat you rough," he said.

When Omar Bradley was graduated from the United States Military Academy, the class prophet wrote the following about him in the West Point year book: "His most prominent characteristic is getting there . . . and if he keeps up the clip he has started, some of us some day will be bragging to our grandchildren that 'Sure, General Bradley was a classmate of mine.' "

That prophecy was strangely accurate, for, in the spring of 1943, Omar Bradley achieved in Tunisia one of the outstanding victories of the war—the victory in which he surrounded and overwhelmed the Germans at Bizerte and captured 37,000 prisoners, with a loss of only 421 lives on our side. He did it by a series of surprises, by secretly moving fifty thousand men, several thousand vehicles, and vast supplies two hundred miles in the darkness and then striking the Germans at places where they least expected a blow. General Bradley used new and unorthodox tactics that had never been described in any military textbooks—tactics that caught the enemy off his guard and sent him reeling into a trap.

A few days later the whole German army in Tunisia collapsed. Thirty-seven thousand Germans captured! Think of it—eighty-eight Germans for every American and Frenchman killed in action. Eighty-eight to one. What a ratio! Yes, General Bradley bought victory in Tunisia at an astounding bargain. In all military history, few victories of such magnitude have 'ever been won with so little loss of life.

That victory was made possible by thirty years of constant study and preparation. During the balmy years of peace that followed the first World War, many army men loafed their time away. But not Omar Bradley. Bradley devoted all of his time

124

Lieutenant-General Bradley

after leaving West Point to studying and teaching military science and to gaining experience. He once said, "I've done every kind of job there is to do in the Army." He certainly got around. During twenty-nine years, he served in thirty-three Army posts.

From 1920 to 1924 he taught mathematics at West Point. This experience helped him to make quick decisions on the battlefield in World War II—quick decisions that smashed the Germans and saved American lives. Sounds absurd, doesn't it? Yet General Bradley himself declared that those four years of teaching mathematics enabled him to think through military problems in one-fourth the time he had formerly required.

General Bradley never smokes, rarely drinks, loves to eat beefsteak at every meal—even for breakfast. He can devour a couple of quarts of ice cream a day.

His favorite music is Negro spirituals and West Point songs like "Brave Old Army Team" and "Alma Mater." His favorite books are *Bob, Son of Battle* and *Ivanhoe*. He reads *Ivanhoe* through almost every year. His wife told me that he is very fond of adventure, western, and detective stories. But much of his reading is devoted to military affairs. He is an authority on the Civil War. He regards Lee as the second greatest general this nation ever produced. The first? Well, he believes first honors should go to General George C. Marshall, Chief of Staff of the United States Army. General Bradley's own career has been deeply influenced by the teaching and example of General Marshall.

I asked Mrs. Bradley to tell me of the biggest mistake her husband had ever made during the twenty-eight years of their married life and she said, "I honestly can't think of any mistakes he has made." Most wives are like that, aren't they—or are they?

I asked her what General Bradley's worst fault was and she replied, "Well, sometimes to me he seems pessimistic; but he says he isn't pessimistic. He says he is merely looking on all sides of a problem." Well, if looking at all sides of a problem is a fault, I wish more of us had it, don't you?

In July, 1944, General Bradley made a prophecy to the war correspondents who were interviewing him. He said, "If I can get three hours of good flying weather any day before lunch, I'll break out of Normandy." He had the power he needed, the men, the supplies, the tanks, the artillery. He knew that if he could have two thousand bombers blast a wide gap in the German lines, he could loose his forces like a devastating tornado.

On July 25, General Bradley got the weather he wanted and the Germans got havoc and hell from the skies. Through the wide gap that our bombers tore in the enemy lines, General Bradley's force rushed like a giant rocket. This rocket, together with our Allied forces, exploded over Brittany and it kept on bursting and exploding across France and into the Reich with such power and brilliance that at times the confused Germans were running in the wrong direction.

And Omar Bradley, the boy who would never have gone to West Point at all if he hadn't been too timid to tell the officer in charge that he had failed in his geometry problem—that boy became America's most successful field commander.

HE KNOWS HOW TO HANDLE SHIPS,
JAPS, AND WIVES

ADMIRAL CHESTER W. NIMITZ BECAME the commander of the greatest fleet the world has ever known, and he also became Commander-in-Chief of the Pacific Ocean Area—an expanse of islands and salt water that is almost twenty-two times as large as the United States, an ocean area far larger than all of North America, South America, Europe, Asia, Africa and Australia combined. He won, at Midway, one of the greatest naval battles in our history; yet when he took command of the Pacific Fleet on the last day of 1941—twenty-four days after Pearl Harbor— he faced the most tragic situation that had ever confronted an American naval officer. We had just suffered the greatest naval defeat in our history.

At five minutes before eight on Sunday morning, December 7, 1941, our Pacific Fleet had eight battleships. Two hours later, five of these eight battleships lay on the bottom of Pearl Harbor, battered by bombs. Among them was Admiral Nimitz' old flagship, the *Arizona*. The three remaining battleships were so severely damaged that they had to be sent home for repairs. It was more than a defeat. It was a major disaster. We knew it. And so did the Japs.

The Japs also knew that our Navy was tragically short of ships, planes, anti-aircraft guns, submarines, ammunition, and all kinds of supplies. But even the Japs would have been astounded had they known that after Pearl Harbor we had only

176 combat planes to protect the entire Pacific Ocean. We knew the Japs would strike again—would strike quickly—while we were still weak.

Under these tragic conditions, President Roosevelt knew that the winning of our war with Japan depended to a large extent on sending the right man to Pearl Harbor. So he chose Admiral Chester W. Nimitz.

The way in which Admiral Nimitz traveled from Washington to Pearl Harbor sounds like an incident out of a detective story or an adventure novel. He carried secret Government documents—secret documents showing the damage inflicted on our Navy by the Japs. The Government knew that Jap agents longed to get hold of that secret report and that the Japs would, if they could, liquidate Admiral Nimitz to get the papers. So, to hide his identity, Admiral Nimitz traveled from Washington to California under the assumed name of "Mr. Wainwright"; and, to further hide his identity, he wore, not his naval uniform, but civilian clothes. Like a fictional detective, he carried his secret papers not in a briefcase, but in an old canvas sewing bag that belonged to his wife.

Why did President Roosevelt select Admiral Nimitz above all other high-ranking naval officers to take charge of our Pacific Fleet immediately after Pearl Harbor? From the standpoint of seniority, he was outranked by twenty-eight other flag officers. He was jumped over the heads of these twenty-eight men and made Commander-in-Chief, not only of our Pacific Fleet but also of our Pacific Ocean Area. He was given this immense power and responsibility largely because he has four outstanding qualities.

First, he has had long experience and knowledge in naval affairs. A few years after leaving Annapolis, he applied for duty on a battleship—an attractive and glamorous assignment. But he got the very opposite of what he was hoping for: he got duty on one of our first crude submarines. He described it as "a cross between a Jules Verne fantasy and a whale." It smelled worse than a whaling station—and what with the gas fumes and battery explosions, it was about as safe as a wounded whale on a rampage.

But in spite of the smell and the danger, Chester W. Nimitz developed a whale of an enthusiasm for the pigboats. This Texas lad, who had never seen salt water until he was sixteen years old, believed that submarines would have a profound effect on naval warfare. So he developed a veritable passion for undersea battleships; and in 1913, when he was only twenty-seven years old, he was already Commander of our submarine forces in the Atlantic; and he served with our undersea forces during the first World War. He later built and commanded our submarine base at Pearl Harbor.

Then he set out to get a rich experience in all kinds of naval activities; he studied Diesel engines in Europe, installed the first Diesel engine in an American naval vessel, and then acted as chief engineer.

He has served in all kinds of capacities on all kinds of vessels from pigboats to battleships. And wherever he served, he was respected for his wide and detailed knowledge and ability. Early in his career, he was commanding an old destroyer that suddenly sprang a leak. The water began flowing in faster than the pumps could take care of it. The chief engineer called excitedly to the bridge: "She is going to sink. What shall I do?"

The future admiral standing on the bridge replied: "Look on Page 84 of Barton's *Engineering Manual;* it tells you what to do in a case like this." The engineer looked. He acted. The boat was saved.

A second quality that explains Admiral Nimitz' success in the Navy is his enthusiasm for everything that floats on salt water. The Admiral himself is the authority for this statement. "I have enjoyed," he says, "every one of my assignments and I believe it has been so because of my making it a point to become as deeply immersed and as interested in each activity as possible."

A third outstanding quality of Admiral Nimitz is his superb ability to lead men. Generous in his praise, he is eager to give credit here, there, and everywhere. There is no man in the Navy more respected or better liked.

Foster Hailey spent almost two years out in the Pacific Ocean. He talked to thousands of naval officers and he said, in an article in the New York *Times,* that he never heard even one of these officers criticize Nimitz, either as a man or an admiral. Foster Hailey goes on to say: "Men who sailed with Nimitz in his days of sea command said he always had a happy ship instead of a taut one and that no efficiency was lost by his ease of command."

A fourth quality that explains the ability of Chester W. Nimitz is his calmness and self-confidence in times of crisis. The way he handled affairs at Pearl Harbor showed that.

When he arrived in Pearl Harbor, hurried and worried Army and Navy officers rushed into his office; but most of them emerged with more ease and confidence. When excited newspaper men pressed him for information about future plans and operations, he replied: "I can best answer those questions by repeating an old saying that they have out here in Hawaii: 'Hoo mana wahui.' It means 'Time will take care of that.' "

It has. Ask the Japs.

Admiral Nimitz has a genius for telling jokes and stories—a talent that makes him popular everywhere. He can give you many reasons why a battleship is called a "she." For one thing, he says, "it costs a lot of money to keep her in paint and powder," and for another "she loves to rest on the bosom of a swell."

When he became a rear-admiral, his wife pleaded with him to stop telling sprightly stories. He did for a while. But then came a day when he had to address a convention of Red Cross nurses in Washington, D. C. The day was hot. The nurses had just finished listening to a long, dry talk. So imagine their surprise when Chester Nimitz, the blue-eyed, white-haired rear-admiral,

Admiral Chester W. Nimitz

arose and told a short, racy tale of the sea. The girls howled for more. So he told another. His wife was seated in a box, listening. She knew what the Admiral could do once he really got warmed up. So she became alarmed. She tried frantically to wave him down. His second story went over well. So did his wife—almost. Suddenly the Admiral sat down. His speech was finished. It may not have been one of the most learned addresses ever given to a Red Cross convention, but it certainly was one of the shortest and most popular.

Admiral Nimitz is courteous under all conditions. After smashing the Jap invasion armada in the battle of Midway, he flew back to the West Coast to confer with Admiral Ernest J. King. As his seaplane landed, he came very near being killed. A drifting log ripped the bottom out of the seaplane, stood it on its nose, and flipped it over on its back. The co-pilot was killed. Two officers were seriously injured. Admiral Nimitz suffered some bruises and sprains. As the survivors were being taken ashore, Admiral Nimitz stood up in the boat. He was wet and dripping. The sailor in charge of the boat hadn't the foggiest idea who he was. So the sailor yelled: "Hey you, sit down!" The Commander-in-Chief of the Pacific Fleet meekly obeyed. The sailor got a second look. His eyes popped. His heart almost stopped. He stuttered. He started to apologize. The Admiral smiled. "Stick to your guns, sailor," he said, "you were right."

Admiral Chester W. Nimitz takes an hour's walk each morning before breakfast, swims a mile once a week, likes to pitch horseshoes, still plays a fair game of tennis, and fires a dozen shots on the pistol range behind his office each morning to keep in practice.

His ability to relax completely has enabled him to carry vast responsibilities that would crush the average man. At noon he takes a long sun bath, occasionally dozing off for a while, but more often holding a conference—in the midst of his sun bath.

131

Biographical Roundup

The night the Breaker's Hotel at Waikiki was opened as a center for enlisted men, the white-haired Admiral Nimitz was photographed dancing with an attractive brunette. The Navy okayed the picture for publicity purposes, but wise old Admiral Nimitz grabbed the first picture himself and rushed it to his wife, airmail, before anyone else could show it to her. That man is not only a naval strategist. He is also a philosopher and a psychologist.

For two years after the disaster at Pearl Harbor, Admiral Nimitz fought a defensive war. But he came to have the mightiest flotilla that ever roamed the sounding seas. And he smashed his way across the Pacific with a speed that astounded the Japs —with a speed that made their buck teeth chatter.

The best description I have ever read of Admiral Nimitz appeared in the year book of his graduating class at Annapolis in 1905. It described him as "a man of cheerful yesterdays and confident tomorrows."

SHE FACED A HUNDRED THOUSAND HOSTILE SOLDIERS TO SAVE HER HUSBAND

IN 1876, A CHINESE BOY in Boston, Massachusetts, ran away from a silk store operated by his uncle. The boy despised business and longed to get an education, but his Chinese uncle was bitterly opposed to such a silly idea, so this twelve-year-old boy slipped out of the store one day, ran down to the Boston Harbor, and hid himself on a steamship which was preparing to nose out to sea.

That Chinese boy was destined to become the father of Madame Chiang Kai-shek, the most influential woman in the world today. In fact he was destined to rear one of the most extraordinary families in Chinese history—the Soong Family. A book of 340 pages was recently written about his three daughters. They rose from obscurity to marry three of China's leaders —in fact they and their husbands have almost created modern China.

One daughter, Chung Ling, married Doctor Sun Yat Sen, China's George Washington, the father of the Chinese Revolution, the man who overthrew the Manchu Dynasty that had ruled China for 268 years, the man who established the Chinese Republic.

Another daughter, E Ling, married Doctor Kung, the Chinese Minister of Finance, a lineal descendant of the greatest man in Chinese history, Confucius.

His third daughter, May Ling—a name which means "Beauti-

ful Life"—married the man who runs China today, Chiang
Kai-shek, the Generalissimo of all China's armies, the dominat-
ing power among China's four hundred million people.

When the boy who was destined to become the father of
Madame Chiang Kai-shek stowed away on a steamship in Boston Harbor, he didn't know where the ship was going and he
didn't care, so long as he got away from his uncle. The captain
of the ship on which he was sailing had the extraordinary name
of Charley Jones. Captain Jones was delighted to find that he
had a Chinese stowaway aboard. He was delighted because he
could use the boy's help in his cabin; and since Captain Jones
was a deeply religious man, he was delighted with the prospect
of converting this boy to Christianity. So every night Captain
Jones read the Bible aloud to the stowaway. When the ship
finally tied up to a wharf in Wilmington, North Carolina, Captain Charley Jones turned the Chinese boy over to Reverend
Ricaud, the pastor of the Fifth Street Southern Methodist
Church in Wilmington.

The boy joined the church and was baptized as—well, his
name was Soong, but he insisted on being baptized *Charley
Jones* Soong, after the good captain who had befriended him
and carried him away to a new world.

The pastor of the Methodist Church was excited about all
this. He felt that God himself had sent this boy to him so that
the boy could be converted and baptized and sent back to Asia
to convert the Chinese to Christianity. So with his heart beating
high, this Methodist preacher rushed down to Durham, North
Carolina, and persuaded General Carr, a rich textile manufacturer and philanthropist, to finance the boy's education at the
Methodist Trinity College, which is now a part of Duke University.

Charley Jones Soong knew that his benefactor had millions
of dollars; but with a fine spirit of independence, he felt that
he ought to make a part of his own expenses through college.

Madame Chiang Kai-shek

So he sold books from door to door and made hammocks and sold them from door to door.

Years later he returned to China and made a fortune by introducing modern machinery into Shanghai. He also printed Bibles and he risked his life by printing revolutionary pamphlets for Dr. Sun Yat Sen.

When Charles Jones Soong sent his three daughters to America to be educated, he defied a sacred tradition that had existed for thousands of years. When his three daughters returned to China, they were the greatest missionaries of America's spirit that we have ever had; and they were probably the greatest missionaries of Christianity since Saint Paul carried Christianity to Rome.

Madame Chiang Kai-shek attended Wesleyan College for Women in Macon, Georgia, the oldest chartered woman's college in the world; and she graduated from Wellesley College in Massachusetts.

Before she left America at the age of nineteen, she said: "The only thing Oriental about me is my face." When she reached Shanghai, she had to take lessons in order to learn to read and speak Chinese.

But the important thing was this: Madame Chiang Kai-shek returned to China on fire with a conviction, an ideal. She was determined to consecrate her life to helping lift the Chinese people out of their age-old dirt and disease and hunger. She put fresh life into the child labor movement and she fought for the rights of Chinese children who were working in factories for ten dollars—now, mind you, not for ten dollars a week or ten dollars a month, but for *ten dollars a year*.

Madame Chiang Kai-shek flew all over China talking to groups of Chinese women and missionaries on the menace of opium, dirt, and disease. She inspired them to start community movements for cleanliness and health. They listened with amazement, with an awe bordering on reverence.

135

She preached the American philosophy of sanitation, education, co-operation, and decent living standards. And to do this, she flew to remote villages in China—flew in spite of the fact that flying made her so sick that she had to lie on the floor of the plane with smelling salts to her nose.

Although Generalissimo Chiang Kai-shek ruled millions of people, he had to spend five years begging his present wife, May Ling, to marry him. She told him she wouldn't marry him unless her mother consented, and her mother refused even to talk to this war lord. Finally, in order to talk to her mother, General Chiang Kai-shek had to follow her to Japan where she had gone for a vacation.

Yes, General Chiang Kai-shek tried for five years to get the consent of Mrs. Charley Jones Soong to marry her daughter, May Ling. Finally, when the General submitted proof that he was divorced from his first wife, and when he promised to read the Bible every day and try to become a Christian, he got her permission; so in 1926 the General and the future Madame Chiang Kai-shek were married in Shanghai, while the soft voice of a Chinese contralto sang "Oh, Promise Me."

Madame Chiang Kai-shek took walks with the General every morning, told him Bible stories, and explained Christianity. He became a Christian two years after their marriage. Now, for the first time in history, China is being ruled by a group of Christians. The effect of this is bound to be far-reaching. Future historians may record it as one of the turning points in the bloody history of Asia.

It is quite probable that Madame Chiang Kai-shek has saved the lives of a hundred thousand American fighting men, for under her influence her husband was able to unite China for the first time in tragic centuries of trouble; and a united China pinned down millions of Japanese troops that might otherwise have swept across the Pacific.

Her influence can best be illustrated by one dramatic incident

136

that occurred at a time when China was torn by internal discord. Her husband was kidnapped by a group of jealous and antagonistic generals—ambitious men who wanted to get rid of him and run China themselves.

He was held prisoner for two weeks; but he refused to give in to his captors' demands. He wouldn't even eat the food his kidnappers gave him. He sternly rebuked his captors, declaring over and over that he would make no compromise, that he would rather die than to be untrue to China. The rebellion in which General Chiang Kai-shek was kidnapped broke out before daylight on December 12, 1936. Chiang Kai-shek fled to a near-by mountain clad only in his nightshirt. He climbed a high wall, slipped and fell thirty feet into a ditch, and wrenched his back so painfully he could hardly walk.

Bullets were whistling over his head—bullets and the clatter of machine guns and the bursting of bombs. Running on, he slipped again and fell into a cave half-hidden by thorny bushes. Twice he struggled to his feet; and twice he fell down exhausted. When the rebellious soldiers captured him, he ordered them with imperial dignity to kill him instantly or treat him with the respect that his position demanded.

The news of his kidnapping fell like a bomb shell on China. School children wept and many soldiers committed suicide. His own armies were lined up ready to march against the city where he was held captive; and his planes were loaded with bombs.

China trembled on the verge of another civil war—and one woman stopped it. One woman alone—Madame Chiang Kai-shek. She stopped his generals from issuing the order to march. It was a turning-point in history.

Chiang Kai-shek had ordered his wife not to come to him. She was repeatedly warned that if she came, she would be killed. But she came anyway, by plane, and she handed a revolver to her companion, ordering him to shoot her if the soldiers tried to seize her.

This one frail woman alone braved the enmity of a hundred thousand mutinous soldiers—and won.

She calmed her husband and persuaded him to eat; and she read the Bible to him until he fell asleep. . . . "A thousand shall fall at thy side, and ten thousand at thy right hand; but it shall not come nigh thee . . ."

For two days she pleaded with his kidnappers, not for her husband but for China; she pleaded to prevent the civil war which was growing nearer hour by hour, because after she had left Nanking, the Government troops had started to march.

The kidnappers released Chiang Kai-shek on Christmas Day, 1936; and in a hundred Chinese cities, flags waved in thanksgiving and firecrackers popped for joy. China was now united by a fervor unknown for centuries. Traitors and patriots, communists and capitalists, were at last united under the leadership of one American-educated Chinese girl and her husband.

Madame Chiang Kai-shek is the soul of China's unity and probably the most important woman in the world.

THE GENERAL WHO CONQUERED ROME STOOD TWENTY-EIGHTH FROM THE BOTTOM OF HIS CLASS AT WEST POINT

WERE YOU EVER ACCUSED of being dumb because you got poor grades in school? If so, pull your chair a little closer. I've got encouraging news for you. I know of a man who was graduated from West Point in 1917 and stood 111th from the top of his class. (Since there were only 139 men in his class that meant that only 28 men got lower grades than he did; and 110 men got better grades.

Yet twenty-six years later he became the youngest Lieutenant-General in the United States Army. In fact he skyrocketed from Lieutenant-Colonel to Lieutenant-General in two years. His name is Clark—Lieutenant-General Mark Wayne Clark. The newspapers always refer to him as Mark W. Clark, but his wife and all his close friends call him by his middle name, Wayne.

When General Clark landed his army on the enemy's shores at Salerno, Italy, on September 11, 1943, he accomplished one of the most difficult operations in the art of war.

Winston Churchill, at the time, declared the Salerno invasion was "the most daring amphibious operation we have launched or which, I think, has ever been launched on a similar scale in war."

General Mark Clark's career is a blazing illustration of the fact that the qualities that make one a leader of men have little to do with one's grades in French grammar or geometry.

Biographical Roundup

I once went up to West Point and spent an afternoon talking to Bill Clark, the son of General Mark Wayne Clark. Bill Clark told me that everybody likes his father. People like him the moment they meet him because they sense somehow that he likes them. General Clark greets you with the same spontaneous warmth that a puppy has; he greets you with an old-fashioned tail-wagging smile and a handshake that generates enthusiasm.

One of General Mark Clark's biggest assets as a leader of men is his genuine interest in other people. His son said to me: "My father never had an enemy in his life. I have never known anyone to say one word against my father. He may get mad at a man, he may dislike what a man does; but he won't hate the man himself." To illustrate that point, Bill Clark told me this story: "My father," he said, "once gave me a beautiful gold watch for my birthday. A year or so later somebody stole it out of my jacket at the gymnasium. We were stationed at the time at Fort Lewis, Washington. Dad watched the pawn shops for months in Tacoma and Olympia, Washington. The thief was caught when he pawned the watch. He was a soldier and Dad brought charges against him. That meant he would be court-martialed and probably kicked out of the Army with a dishonorable discharge. Dad knew that a dishonorable discharge would leave a black mark on the man's record for life, and Dad's heart was too soft for that; he withdrew the charges and told the man's company commander that he could handle the problem in any way he saw fit."

No matter how busy General Mark Clark is, he always finds time to do little thoughtful things for other people. For example, during the strain of the North African campaign Mark Clark found time to write a letter of birthday greeting to one of his assistants, Major Paul Revere.

I asked Bill Clark if his father did that sort of thing frequently and he replied, "Yes, practically everything Dad does is out of pure thoughtfulness for others."

General Mark Clark is thoughtful and considerate in the very place where thoughtfulness and unselfishness are needed most —in the home. Bill Clark told me that his father loved to cook and that he had often seen his father order his mother out of the kitchen and then cook and serve the entire meal himself— and, girls, get this: he also washed and dried the dishes himself! Not so bad for a husband who first met his wife on a blind date!

Yes, Mark Wayne Clark met a blonde on a blind date about twenty years ago. She was from Muncie, Indiana, and her name was Maurine Doran. It was not a case of love at first sight—far from it. At first they took little interest in each other. However, she did take a trip with his parents to Panama. Down there in the tropics a handsome aviator fell in love with this Indiana blonde and proposed to her. When she returned to New York, Mark Clark met her at the boat and heard the shocking news—Maurine was engaged to another man. "I guess competition was what he needed," said Mrs. Mark Clark, as she told the story, "for he proposed a few days later and I accepted." On Mark Clark's table, wherever he is, are pictures of the girl he met on a blind date twenty years ago and their two children, Bill and Patricia Ann.

General Clark demands exactness in everything. Mrs. Clark always keeps a monthly record of household expenses, and if the figures are off-balance by even ten cents, Mark Clark will spend an hour trying to discover what happened to that ten cents. He doesn't care about the ten cents, but he can't tolerate books that don't balance.

When General Clark's son was preparing for his West Point examinations, his father said to him over and over: "Check your facts, son. Check your facts. Do your mathematical problems twice or three times to check the results."

Biographical Roundup

Bill Clark once handed his father a school report carrying a grade of 99. His father asked Bill if he was satisfied with a grade like that. Bill said, "Yes, aren't you?" General Clark answered, "Well, it isn't 100." Bill replied, "Dad, you wouldn't be satisfied unless I got 110."

I asked Bill Clark if his father ever admitted that he himself didn't make a brilliant record at West Point. Bill Clark said, "No, I didn't know a thing about Dad's record at West Point until I heard one of his classmates mention it one day. I was astonished to hear it."

General Clark is a modest man. He never brags about his accomplishments. One day Bill Clark was in his father's room while his father was changing his undershirt. Bill was surprised to see a scar on his father's back—a scar a foot long and half an inch wide. He was surprised because his father had never mentioned it. When Bill inquired about the scar, General Clark replied casually, "Oh, I was wounded by shrapnel in the last war." That was all, no details, no talking about how brave he was. Bill never discovered the facts until six months later. Then one day, while rummaging through some old books in the attic, he discovered that his father had been awarded the purple heart and cited for bravery under fire.

General Mark Clark smoked for ten years; and then he suddenly gave it up because the girl that he met on a blind date—his wife—complained about the odor of cigars.

What do you suppose is his favorite drink? Milk. In peace times he drinks milk three times a day—about two quarts every twenty-four hours.

His classmates at West Point gave Mark Clark the nickname of "Contraband" because he was always bringing contraband food to his room. The cadets weren't allowed to bring perishable food out of the mess hall, but Mark Wayne Clark stood six feet two and he had the appetite of two horses and a white mule. He could never eat enough in the mess hall to tide him over to the next meal. So he would pack sandwiches and meat and cake into the top of his big hat, then put his hat on his head, and march to his room with this "contraband" cargo of food. That happened a quarter of a century ago, but General Clark's son told me that his father is still hungry. He said, "You will usually find a couple of candy bars on his desk today." In fact General Clark has such an appetite that when he is invited out to dinner, he eats a light meal at home two hours before dinner is to be served. A light meal of soup, sandwiches, milk, and ice cream. He eats that to tide him over until dinner time two hours later.

His favorite food is a very thick, rare steak with boiled potatoes. He is so interested in food that he has trained himself to be an expert cook.

Bill Clark told me that his Dad can forgive almost everything except deception and lying. He said to his son: "Bill, always tell the whole truth and never under any circumstances leave out any unpleasant details because they might reflect on you."

Before leaving West Point, I said to Bill Clark, "You have been telling me a lot about your Dad's good points; now tell me what is his worst fault."

"Temper," said Bill. "He has a bad temper at times. He can be mean for a little while, but he can't keep it up for long. He is too soft-hearted for that. After losing his temper, he always apologizes and tries to do something nice for you to make up for his outburst."

General Clark is extremely fond of dogs. He has had five cocker spaniels, one bulldog, one police dog, and two chows. One night he lost his temper and punished one of the dogs because he had taken a bite out of a costly fur coat belonging to one of the guests. Bill Clark told me that after the company left that night, he went out into the kitchen and there was his father holding the dog on his lap, petting him, and saying, "I'm so sorry, boy, I shouldn't have done that. I'll never do it again.

Please forgive me." One look at the dog, said Bill, was enough to convince him that his father had already been forgiven.

Bill Clark went into his father's room one day and saw a book lying open on his desk. The book was entitled *Daily Word*. This book is a collection of inspirational messages and verses from the Bible. Bill Clark was surprised. He had never heard his father say anything about being religious. He asked his mother about it and she said, "Yes, your father reads the Bible often and prays every night before he goes to bed."

The day the Fifth Army landed in Italy, General Clark opened his *Daily Word,* and the message printed for that day read:

"Though a thousand foes surround,
Safe with Thee I shall be found."

THE MOST FAMOUS BALL CLUB MANAGER IN
AMERICA LOST EIGHT HUNDRED GAMES
IN EIGHT YEARS

HAVE YOU EVER HEARD of Cornelius McGillicuddy? Sure you have. He is the best loved man in baseball. Cornelius McGillicuddy has been in professional baseball since 1883. He has been both a player and a manager, and he is known and loved wherever baseball is played. But he is known, not by his real name—Cornelius McGillicuddy—but as Connie Mack.

Connie Mack has done more for the game of baseball than any other man who ever lived. He entered the game when it was rough, rowdy, disreputable, and not too honest. By precept and example, he helped to clean up the game, keep it decent and respectable, and make it the national game of 130 million people.

He was born in 1862, away back when a prairie lawyer from Illinois by the name of Lincoln was in the White House. Today he can toss a baseball around better than lots of youngsters, in spite of the fact that he has been doing it for—well, Connie himself doesn't remember exactly how long, but for well over seventy years.

Connie Mack told me, when I interviewed him, that his life had really been an almost unbroken holiday. He said that he had never ceased to be astonished over the fact that people are willing to pay grown men to do something that is so much fun.

When Connie Mack was twenty years old, his father died; so Connie had to quit school and get a factory job to support the

145

family. He worked in a shoe factory for ten dollars a week. Each morning he walked three miles to the shoe factory, and each night he walked three miles home—a total of six miles—in order to save ten cents carfare to give his mother.

Connie Mack despised making shoes and he loved baseball; so he made a wise decision: he decided to make his living doing the thing he loved to do. But his mother didn't think it was a wise decision. She was shocked; and she had a right to be shocked, for he was the main support of the family. The job he gave up paid him cash on the barrel-head every Saturday night. How much salary do you suppose he was paid each week as a professional baseball player? Nothing. Absolutely nothing. How then did he and his family manage to eat? Well, Connie Mack, as he looks back at it now, wonders himself how they did it. That first job of his was with the East Brookfield team of the Central Massachusetts League. Nobody on that team got any salary because the team had no regular source of income. There was no admission charged to see the game. They played on vacant lots, and as they ran after balls they stumbled over tin cans, scrap iron, and old discarded horse collars. When the game was over, they passed the hat and took up a collection. At least they tried to pass it, but Connie Mack told me that as soon as they started to take up the collection, the crowd melted like snow upon the desert's dusty face. Each Saturday night Connie Mack got his share of the nickels, dimes, and quarters that had been thrown into the hat. Just that and nothing more. Sometimes when the finances got too desperate, the ball team would replenish their exchequer by putting on a strawberry festival or a clambake.

For years Connie Mack was a catcher. He stood away back behind the batter and caught the balls on the first bounce. Any catcher who used a glove in those days was regarded as a sissy. And here's one for the book: until 1880, a foul ball caught on the first bounce was out.

146

Connie Mack

What is the secret of Connie Mack's astounding success as a baseball manager? Eddie Collins has answered that question and Eddie ought to know what he is talking about, for he played under Connie Mack's management for many years. He is now Vice President and Business Manager of the Boston Americans. Eddie Collins says that Connie Mack's success was not due to his superior knowledge of the technique of baseball. "The whole secret of Connie Mack's success," says Collins, "is that he understands people and knows how to lead and inspire men. You would have to comb the world to find another man with Connie Mack's ability to make human beings extend themselves."

Of course Connie Mack is Irish and you might figure that he was born with the ability to inspire men to extend themselves. The fact is, however, that during his first three years as baseball manager, he made a poor showing. One year his team ended up in sixth place, the next year in seventh place, and the next year in last place. But Connie Mack differed from most men: he didn't blame his players for this poor showing; he figured that probably *he* was to blame. He figured that he didn't know how to handle men. After Connie Mack had been managing a major league team for three years, he voluntarily gave up his job and dropped back as player-manager of the Milwaukee team—a job that would give him the time and opportunity to study the problem of getting men to do what he wanted them to do.

When he came back to the major leagues again, he handled the players so successfully that he developed the best teams the diamond had ever known up to that time. He won more pennants and more World Championships than any other team up to the days of the modern New York Yankees.

Connie Mack's biggest asset is his ability to arouse enthusiasm among his men. How does he do it? He has a genuine liking for people. It isn't synthetic. It's the real McCoy. "I always try," Connie Mack told me, "to say a good word for everybody."

147

He never tears a player down, but always tries to build him up. He teaches and leads men by suggestion and encouragement rather than by fault-finding and nagging. For example, when Eddie Collins joined the Athletics, fresh from college, he had a lot to learn about sliding bases. Connie said to Eddie, "Did you ever notice how Cobb slides? Pretty nice sliding, isn't it?" Eddie hadn't noticed it up to that time, but he did afterwards. He practiced the Cobb slide hour after hour, day after day, and finally became one of the game's best base runners.

Connie told me of another important rule he uses in managing men. Never, never, under any circumstances whatever does he call a player's attention to his mistakes in front of the other players or in front of strangers. Connie Mack says: "Criticizing a man in front of a third party doesn't breed co-operation. It breeds rebellion."

Connie told me that he learned by hard experience that it is always advisable to wait twenty-four hours before calling a player's attention to his mistakes. He didn't do that in his early days as a manager. In those days he used to undress and dress with his players. If the team had lost, he found it impossible to refrain from criticizing the players and from wrangling and arguing with them bitterly over the defeat. Since he couldn't be sure of controlling himself and his tongue immediately after the game, he made it a rule not to see the players at all after a game, nor to discuss the defeat until the next day.

Connie refrains from bossing his men too much, too. He lets his older players work out their own problems in their own way. He has discovered that what is good for one man is not necessarily good for another.

For example, back in 1913 Connie Mack had the pennant race won, well before the season ended, and he decided that his two great pitchers, Plank and Bender, ought to rest up for the World Series. Mack gave them ten days off—but he did not tell them what to do.

Connie Mack

How did they spend those ten days? Bender gave all his ten days to baseball. He went to the park every day, worked out, and jogged around the lot. He lived, slept, and ate baseball. Plank did just the opposite for ten days. He refused to touch a baseball. Instead, he went to his farm near Gettysburg and fished and loafed. Both men were veterans. Each one knew what he needed personally to get ready for the World's Series. Both were in perfect condition when the series started and they pitched amazing baseball.

Although Connie Mack has been one of the most successful managers in baseball history, he has often tasted the dregs of defeat. He is the only manager who ever finished in last place for seven consecutive years, and he is the only manager who ever lost eight hundred games in eight years.

Does he worry? Not now, but he used to. He told me that after a series of disastrous defeats, he used to worry for days—so much he could hardly eat or sleep. Then he stopped. That was a quarter of a century ago; and he hasn't worried since.

I asked Connie Mack how he manages to avoid worry. "I discovered," he replied, "that worry was threatening to wreck my career as a baseball manager. I honestly believe," he said, "that if I had gone on worrying I would probably be in my grave today. I saw how foolish it was; and I forced myself to get so busy thinking and preparing to *win* games in the future that I had no time left to worry over the ones that were already lost. You can't grind grain," Connie Mack said, "with water that has already gone down the creek."

Many people are in a rut by the time they are forty, but Connie Mack, in his eighties, fights to keep out of a rut. He is fighting it so hard that he won't even permit himself to go through the same streets every day on his way to the office. Now and then he deliberately chooses different ways.

Connie Mack told me that he attributes his years of good health to several factors:

149

Biographical Roundup

He inherited a good strong constitution and he takes plenty of rest. He sleeps ten hours a night and also takes a nap every afternoon. If the team is playing at home, he goes to the private office in the ball park, locks the door, disconnects the telephone, and takes a nap for twenty or thirty minutes.

He eats carefully and manages to keep his weight down to 155 pounds—and, mind you, he is six feet two inches tall.

He used to drink occasionally. Then one day Connie Mack had a family party, with seven children and sixteen grandchildren. Connie had had a couple of highballs and his sons were teasing him about being a heavy drinker. He picked up a glass of beer at the table and said, "You are now going to watch the old man take his last drink." They did. That was in 1937. He hasn't taken a drink since.

Connie Mack was born during the Civil War, yet he is not thinking of retiring. "I'm not rich," he told me. "I can't afford to retire. I have to keep going. But I am going to retire," he added, "as soon as I begin telling the same stories over and over. When I begin that, I'll know that I am old."

THEY SAID HE WOULD TEACH HISTORY; INSTEAD, HE MAKES HISTORY FOR OTHERS TO TEACH

IN THE EARLY YEARS of this century a high-school boy wandered into the office of a weekly newspaper in Kansas—the Abilene *News*—and picked up a book belonging to Editor J. W. Howe. This book told the thrilling experiences of one of the great military leaders of all time—Hannibal. As the boy read, he became completely absorbed in the story of Hannibal, who crossed the Alps with elephants and fought the Italians for fifteen years. This Kansas boy became so fascinated with military history that he devoured Gibbon's *Decline and Fall of the Roman Empire* and then spent months poring over books on American history—reading biographies of Lee, Grant, Washington, Stonewall Jackson. He became so fascinated with history, especially military history, that the yearbook of the Abilene high school prophesied that someday he would be a professor of history at Yale. That prophecy was just a bit off-center. He never *taught* history at Yale, but he did *make* history that other people will be teaching at Yale a good many years from now. Yes, he has made history that will have a far more profound effect on mankind than Hannibal and his elephants ever did. That boy's name was Dwight David Eisenhower, or "Ike," as his friends call him.

Yes, Ike Eisenhower, the peace-loving boy from the wheat-fields of Abilene, Kansas, was to direct the forces that will decide the fate of 300,000,000 people in Western Europe.

Biographical Roundup

It was at four o'clock in the morning of June 5, 1944, that General Eisenhower decided to invade Europe the next day. His decision was made in the sitting room of a charming country home somewhere in England. It was made after thirty minutes of conversation with the men in charge of the air, naval, and ground forces; and with the weather experts. Two days previously, General Eisenhower had given the order to start the invasion immediately. Then half an hour later he had canceled the order. The weather had changed. Now the weather seemed more propitious. Further delay might take the fine edge off the morale of the troops who were already on board the ships, waiting and eager to go. After weighing, with his usual care, all the facts involved, pro and con, General Eisenhower said: "In view of all these factors, I think we had better go ahead."

That one sentence, spoken without enthusiasm or excitement, launched the greatest amphibian force ever known in the long, bloody history of warfare. Ike Eisenhower, the boy who used to wash dishes and milk cows in Kansas, was to wield an influence such as had never before been placed in the hands of one man. He was to be the Supreme Commander of all the forces on the Allied Western Front—the infantry, the artillery, the engineers, the navy, and the bombers roaring overhead. Yes, Ike Eisenhower was to command an army far greater than the combined infantry of Napoleon, Julius Caesar, Hannibal, and Charlemagne all put together. He was to command a fleet greater than all the navies commanded by Nelson, Hawkins, Drake, John Paul Jones, and Admiral Dewey combined.

And he was to command by far the greatest assembly of air power that has ever been dreamed of.

Yet he handled all this crushing responsibility with the quiet calm made possible by years of training, by vast preparations complete to the smallest particular, and by an incredible accumulation of all the materials of war.

152

General Dwight D. Eisenhower

His formula for military success is severely simple. He says: "Plan to the least detail. Then strike like death itself." His experts did plan to the least detail. For example, eight hundred typewritten pages were required to set down the details of only the navy's part in the invasion. One complete set of the navy's orders and maps for the invasion weighed three hundred pounds.

Ike Eisenhower's name was inscribed on a bronze tablet at West Point twenty-eight years ago. It was inscribed there because of his outstanding success as a football player. He was called "the Kansas Cyclone" because he tore down the football field like a tornado sweeping everything out of his path. Eisenhower's football career at West Point was ended by a broken knee. His career in Europe will be ended only by a broken Hitler and a broken Germany.

When it came to selecting a Supreme Commander for our invasion forces, Ike Eisenhower was the first choice, not only of President Roosevelt and Winston Churchill, but also of Stalin. In fact, Eisenhower used to keep on his office desk in England a handwritten letter that President Roosevelt had sent to Stalin assuring him that Ike Eisenhower would be Supreme Commander of our invasion forces.

Yet when Eisenhower first wanted to go to West Point thirty-four years ago, his family was shocked—shocked because they had belonged for generations to a religious sect opposing all wars. It was called the United Brethren of Christ. Ike Eisenhower's grandfather had been a preacher in that church, delivering his sermons in the German language. His own mother and father had first met while attending a little college conducted by the United Brethren of Christ. So you can imagine how startled and stunned they were to discover that their third son wanted to become a soldier. But Dwight Eisenhower had made up his mind; and no amount of pleading by his parents could persuade him to change.

Biographical Roundup

At first, he had planned to go to Annapolis and become a naval officer. His boyhood chum, Everett Hazlett, was going there and Dwight Eisenhower would undoubtedly have gone there too, except for one little oversight. He neglected to take the examination until he had passed his twentieth birthday, and he was too old then.

General Eisenhower's astonishingly rapid rise in the Army was due to his knowledge, his training, his judgment, his character, his ability to get things done, and, above all else, his ability to lead men. A leader has been defined as a man who can persuade others to do things without fear of punishment or hope of reward. General Eisenhower has that quality to an extraordinary degree. Everyone likes him. He is often called "the Army's favorite general." He radiates that indefinable quality called personality.

His wife says, "Ike has the most engaging grin I ever saw." And she adds, "Ike is a brilliant conversationalist. He is informed on almost everything. It is a joy to hear him talk. I have lived with him for a good many years and he still fascinates me." Testimony like that, coming from a wife, is rarer than pigeon-blood rubies.

Winston Churchill once said to Eisenhower: "What I like about you, Ike, is you ain't no glory-hopper." Yea, verily, those are his exact words. Churchill, a man who revels in rhetoric, also enjoys collecting specimens of picturesque American slang. Admiral Cunningham once heard Eisenhower say to a man in North Africa: "What I like about you is you ain't no glory-hopper," and the Admiral repeated the remark to Churchill. Later Churchill in turn repeated Eisenhower's own words to Eisenhower himself.

Dwight Eisenhower certainly ain't no glory-hopper. He ain't never tried to hop on the bandwagon or hog the limelight. He cares about as little for personal glory as Abe Lincoln did. He refuses to wear medals, seldom wears military ribbons. He re-

154

General Dwight D. Eisenhower

fused to waste his time in England attending even important social affairs, and he insisted that his headquarters be referred to as "Allied Force Headquarters" instead of "Eisenhower's Headquarters."

He never drinks; says he has had to carry too much secret information in his head to trust his tongue under the influence of liquor. In peace times he loves to play bridge and poker; and he usually wins, especially at poker, for he knows all the percentages of the game and he can read human nature.

His knowledge of military history is phenomenal. During the campaign in North Africa, someone asked him about Hannibal's campaign in Italy. Eisenhower astonished his listeners by discussing Hannibal's campaign in detail for forty minutes. A member of his staff felt that Eisenhower couldn't possibly remember so many details of battles fought two hundred years before Christ was born; so he checked the facts and found that Eisenhower was correct. Eisenhower has devoted most of his spare time since he left West Point to studying military history and military problems.

He is a rapid reader. His son told me that in peace time General Eisenhower reads a stack of Western stories magazines through in one night. But when he flew to England to take command of our European forces, Eisenhower took only one book with him on the plane. That book was the Bible.

Eisenhower usually works sixteen to eighteen hours a day, says he needs only five hours sleep, and is usually up at daybreak. That is nothing new for him. When he was a boy back in Kansas, he used to get up at half-past four on winter mornings—get up in a cold house when the thermometer was 20 degrees below zero, light a fire in the kitchen stove, and cook breakfast for the family.

And speaking of cooking, General Eisenhower has always had an enthusiastic interest in good eating. His mother had six sons and no daughters; so he often had to help his mother in the

155

kitchen. John Eisenhower told me that his father is proud of his ability to cook, especially of his ability to make potato salad and vegetable soup—he claims to make the best vegetable soup on earth. He has been known to chase his wife out of the kitchen, cook and serve the entire meal himself, and wash the dishes afterwards. . . . No wonder his wife thinks he is a good conversationalist!

General Eisenhower didn't get the highest grades in West Point. He stood sixty-first from the top in a class of 164; but he did achieve at West Point something infinitely more important than high grades. He achieved vision. He saw years ago that another world war was coming, and he talked about it so much that he was nicknamed "Calamity Ike." He also saw that the airplane and the tank would revolutionize warfare. He wanted to join the air corps right then, but his bride objected. So he went in for tanks and organized the first tank corps the United States Army ever had. He was made Lieutenant-Colonel of the tank corps on his twenty-eighth birthday. He and his new tank unit were aboard a transport ready to sail for Europe on November 11, 1918, when the war suddenly ended.

Now here is an extraordinary fact about General Eisenhower. Though he has directed the most powerful combination of sea, air, and ground forces that the world has ever seen, he himself has never led even a platoon into battle. Hundreds of thousands of our GI Joes have had more actual battle experience than General Eisenhower has had. His job was not to get out where the shells were bursting. His job was to co-ordinate and direct the generals and admirals who were running the show.

General Eisenhower's real name, of course, is Dwight David Eisenhower; and his mother has always objected strenuously to the nickname "Ike." Once when General Eisenhower's wife sent his mother a letter saying that she and Ike were traveling and hoped to stop off in Abilene, Mother Eisenhower replied that she was looking forward to seeing them, but would like to know "who is this 'IKE' with whom you are traveling."

General Eisenhower's mother, well up in years, was still living in Abilene when we entered the war. One day as she sat by her window watching boys in uniform march down the street, she murmured to her companion, "I have got a boy in the Army, too."

Yes. Mother Eisenhower, you've got a boy in the Army, too.

HE DICTATES IN TAXICABS AND TRAVELS
FIVE THOUSAND MILES FOR ONE
WEEK OF SKIING

ONE SPRING DAY IN 1916 my telephone rang and a man who
was studying law and teaching at Princeton University asked
for an appointment. He wanted someone to help him in the
preparation and delivery of an illustrated address on Alaska.
When.I met him the next day, I was immensely impressed, because that young man possessed just about everything necessary
for success—an attractive personality, contagious enthusiasm,
astonishing energy, and boundless ambition. I prophesied then
that someday he would be both rich and famous.

Now my prophecies very often go wrong, but, for once, I was
right. That man became almost an American institution. As
far as riches are concerned—well, his income is a secret, of
course, but *Time Magazine* once estimated that he earned
about 200,000 dollars a year.

His name is Lowell Jackson Thomas, but his wife and his
intimate friends call him "Tommy." Tommy has been broadcasting the news to the Eastern half of the United States five
days a week, without a break, since 1930—an all-time record for
a daily sponsored network program. Also, since 1934 he has
been giving the news to the nation every week through the Fox
Movietone Newsreel.

During those years of broadcasting, Lowell Thomas has said
"So long until tomorrow" thousands of times, and has spoken
millions of words—enough to fill nearly a hundred books.

When I first met Lowell Thomas, he was giving travel talks

158

on Alaska for a few dollars a night, as a sideline to his work at Princeton. I have watched him climb from those days of obscurity up to the top of the ladder. Yet he is still the same modest, sincere, unaffected, considerate man today that he was when I first knew him. In all those years I have never heard anyone criticize Lowell Thomas for anything. If he has even one enemy in this world, I don't know who it is.

Lowell Thomas' life was deeply influenced by his mother and his father. Both had been teachers, but his father finally gave up teaching for medicine. His father, by the way, although in his seventies, is still practicing medicine in Asbury Park, New Jersey, and has recently been handling the medical and surgical problems for an immense naval project.

When Tommy was a boy, his imagination was fired by the travel and adventure stories of Marco Polo, Magellan, Daniel Boone, and Robinson Crusoe. He resolved then that someday he, too, would travel to the far corners of the earth and would set his adventures down in books. Few men have ever been so successful as Lowell Thomas in transferring their dream castles into the stern stuff of reality.

He spent years roaming over Europe, Asia, Alaska, and Australia. He toured India with the Prince of Wales and was the first American traveler ever officially invited to enter and photograph the wild country of Afghanistan. The Governments of India and Burma and the Federated Malay States gave him special trains and river boats and placed strings of elephants at his command, so that he could explore and photograph their strange sights and customs.

He has written over forty books whose very titles ring with the spirit of adventure—books with titles such as *With Lawrence in Arabia, Beyond the Khyber Pass, Pageant of Adventure,* and *These Men Shall Never Die.*

Even as a boy, Lowell Thomas dreamed not only of traveling, but also of lecturing about his travels. He knew that in order to accomplish that ambition, he would have to get an education. He went in for schooling on a large scale, acquiring four college degrees from four educational institutions: Valparaiso University, the University of Denver, Kent College of Law in Chicago, and Princeton University.

He didn't have the money to attend one university, let alone four. During his summer vacations he punched cattle and pitched alfalfa on the Ute Indian Reservation. He worked as a gold miner in Cripple Creek, Colorado. Later he worked as a cub reporter on Denver and Chicago newspapers.

He paid for his board and room during the winter by caring for furnaces and acting as a waiter and as a short-order cook in a restaurant. He fed and milked a cow for one of his professors. He sold real estate. He did a bit of teaching and lecturing on the side.

Back in 1915 the first World War stopped all tourist travel to Europe. That gave Lowell Thomas an idea: why not prepare illustrated talks on the scenic wonders of America? It was a good idea, but it required cash for railroad fares, hotels, photography. Lowell Thomas had no money, but he did have a contagious enthusiasm that has made him one of the best salesmen in America. He persuaded railroad and steamship companies to send him on a de luxe tour, with all expenses paid, throughout the West and up into Alaska. I heard Tommy's address on Alaska; it was full of sweep and gusto and his pictures were superb.

Franklin K. Lane, Secretary of the Interior in President Wilson's Cabinet, also heard that speech. He was instantly captivated. When America declared war on Germany in 1917, Lane persuaded President Wilson to send Lowell Thomas abroad to take pictures of the war and then to return with a series of illustrated productions that would arouse the fighting spirit of the folks back home.

160

Lowell Thomas

There was only one catch to the appointment, but it was a serious one: the job carried no salary and no expense money.

Lowell Thomas induced a group of eighteen millionaires in Chicago to lend him 100,000 dollars to finance his trip abroad to take pictures of the first World War. Eighteen months later he returned to the United States with colored and motion pictures of the fighting, not only in France, Belgium, Italy, and the Balkans, but also of General Allenby's picturesque campaign in the Holy Land—a campaign that swept the Turks out of Jerusalem, Jericho, Bethlehem, and Nazareth, and knocked Turkey out of the war. What was even more sensational, he brought back the story of the most picturesque and romantic figure produced by the first World War—Lawrence of Arabia, the young, shy, silent archeologist who organized the sheiks of the Arabian desert into a guerrilla force which dynamited Turkish railroads and lines of communication.

Lowell Thomas' illustrated talks were presented at the largest theater in New York City for months. Later he was invited to London, where he, an American, told the British people the story of their own astonishing campaign in the Near East.

I had the privilege of being associated with Lowell Thomas at the time, in a business way. I saw London crowds stand in line for hours to buy tickets to hear him. That happened night after night, month after month. He gave his lectures in the Covent Garden Opera House; the demand for seats was so great that the Grand Opera season of London was put off for a month so that Tommy could continue his lectures. Then he moved to Royal Albert Hall, where he addressed from fifteen to twenty-five thousand people every day. The British had never even heard of Lawrence of Arabia until Lowell Thomas told them his thrilling story.

For ten years Tommy continued giving these illustrated talks all over the world. He spoke to four million people, face to

161

face, in more than four thousand audiences in every English-speaking country on the globe.

Then in 1930 Lowell Thomas got the biggest break of his life: an opportunity to broadcast the day's news, daily, for the *Literary Digest*. That was what started him toward his position of prominence in the world of affairs. Tommy gave ten broadcasts each week, and then stayed up all night, two nights a week, doing the Fox Movietone Newsreel. He also answered a vast amount of mail and turned out a book or two each season.

How could he possibly do it all? The answer is that he built a capable organization around himself; and, in addition, Tommy knew how to make every minute count. I was with him one time in London when he was leaving for Australia. He not only dictated letters to his secretary in the taxicab as we were driving to the ship, but he stood on the dock, dictating letters across a fence. He was still dictating letters two minutes before the gangplank was hauled up.

Lowell Thomas doesn't give a hoot for night clubs, parties, or society. His hobbies are horseback riding, softball, and skiing. Skiing isn't a hobby with him—it's an obsession. During the winters he sometimes travels five thousand miles for one week of skiing.

Lowell Thomas married Frances Ryan, a girl of exquisite charm whom he met at the University of Denver. They have one son, Lowell Thomas, Junior, who is already a world traveler and an explorer. He is also a ski expert who has outstripped his dad.

Lowell Thomas one evening found himself in front of the microphone with five pages of his news broadcast missing. That meant his broadcast was about five minutes short, and the time had to be filled in by a studio musician. The catastrophe had been caused by the oversight of a secretary. But Lowell Thomas didn't scold her. When she began to apologize, he told her to forget it. He assured her that her batting average was excellent

162

and that nothing else counted. Tommy never raises his voice or loses his temper. He is an expert in the fine art of human relations.

One day, many years ago, while he was giving a series of illustrated lectures in Boston, a group of angry creditors swooped down on him at the end of a performance. At that period of his career he was not only dead broke, but he faced pressing obligations that he couldn't possibly discharge at once. It's true he had made a fortune. He had grossed a million dollars in one year while still in his twenties. But, through a series of unfortunate reverses, he had also lost a fortune. These creditors and their attorneys were determined to take possession of his camera, films, and projection equipment. Thomas received them as though they had been honored guests, served them tea in his dressing room, sympathized with them, and then pointed out in his sincere, gracious manner that his only hope of paying them soon was to continue what he was doing. The creditors had arrived irritated and angry. They left feeling that they were personal friends of Lowell Thomas. But here is the real point of the story: he later paid them every single cent he owed them! That's "Tommy" for you. -

HE WENT DOWN TO THE SEA IN A DIVER'S HELMET AND BROUGHT UP A DRYDOCK

CAPTAIN EDWARD ELLSBERG OF THE United States Navy is a man whose specialty is accomplishing the impossible. For years, Captain Ellsberg has been doing things that the experts said couldn't be done. Let me illustrate:

Back in 1926, the submarine *S-51*, weighing a thousand tons, was sunk in 132 feet of water off Rhode Island. No submarine had ever before been raised from that depth in the open sea, and most of the experts said it couldn't be done. But Captain Ellsberg did it.

When Edward Ellsberg graduated from the United States Naval Academy in 1914, no midshipman up to that time had ever gotten a perfect grade in navigation. The experts said it couldn't be done. But he did it.

When the United States Navy asked Captain Ellsberg to salvage the sunken drydocks and the sunken Axis ships in the Italian naval base at Massawa in the Red Sea, the experts said— well, let me read to you one sentence from a letter written by Admiral Harold R. Stark, Commander of U. S. Naval Forces in Europe. Admiral Stark said: "At Massawa Captain Ellsberg, by great skill and unflagging energy, raised the two Italian floating docks, in spite of considerable weight of opinion that this was impossible."

Captain Ellsberg's feat of salvage at the Red Sea naval base of Massawa was so extraordinary that the United States Navy awarded him the medal of the Legion of Merit. Many newspapers have declared his salvage work at Massawa was an important factor in the war in the Mediterranean.

That happened in the spring of 1942, six months after Pearl Harbor, in one of the darkest periods of the war. The Germans under Rommel had already driven to within two hundred miles of the Suez Canal and they were bombing the daylights out of Britain's great naval base at Alexandria. The British knew that unless the Germans were prevented from capturing the Suez Canal and the Middle East, the Allied Nations might lose the war.

The British ships were penned up in the eastern Mediterranean and they needed overhauling and repairs badly. Many of their ships were reduced to half-speed because of the thick crust of barnacles on their hulls. But the nearest drydock and repair station was four thousand miles away in South Africa—a distance greater than that between New York and London.

To be sure, the British had conquered Massawa on the Red Sea, only nine hundred miles from Cairo. That base had once had excellent drydocks and naval repair shops. But the defeated Italians swore that if they couldn't use these naval repair shops themselves, they were going to wreck them so completely that nobody else could, either. Before retreating, they smashed the machines with sledge hammers, bombed and sank the great drydocks, and scuttled twenty-six Axis ships in the harbor.

The British knew that if they could repair the naval base at Massawa, it might mean the difference between defeat and victory.

But how could they? The job meant men and materials, and they then had neither. They appealed to the United States for help, and we sent them Captain Ellsberg.

Certain British experts considered the plan to raise the large drydock impracticable. It was obvious that it would take years for all the divers that could be brought to the task to patch the holes in that drydock and pump it dry. Captain Ellsberg, however, with thirteen men, raised it in nine days!

Sounds incredible and it is incredible, especially when you consider all the hardships under which they worked. They worked under the same hardships in reconditioning the sabotaged Italian machine shops and putting them in operation.

First, there was a lack of tools. The defeated Italian Army not only wrecked the machines, but also carried away all the tools. "We were so desperate for tools," Captain Ellsberg told me, "that whenever a ship came into the harbor, we would beg the captain to give us even a hammer or a screwdriver." Ellsberg drove eighty miles to get a couple of carpenter's handsaws; and he salvaged some electric motors from an abandoned gold mine in the hills.

Ellsberg found that the Italians had not smashed the same parts on every motor in the machine shops and that by matching up undamaged parts, he could reassemble about 25 per cent of the original power plant. He and his men set up a crude foundry of their own to replace broken parts. In two months he had nearly every machine in the machine, the carpenter, and the steel-plate shops back in operation.

Another big obstacle was the blistering heat. The Red Sea is the hottest ocean in the world. The sea water was so hot at Massawa that men couldn't go swimming to cool off. The iron plates on the ships sometimes reached a temperature of 160 degrees. An iron tool left in the sun would get so hot that a workman would have to put on a glove before he could pick it up, and he would then have to douse it in the sea before he could use it.

Within six months after Captain Ellsberg had raised the drydock at Massawa, he had repaired three of the four cruisers comprising the whole British fleet operating in the Mediterranean, and had reconditioned eighty other ships in time for the November offensive against Rommel.

Captain Edward Ellsberg

Yes, Captain Ellsberg and his men at Massawa, with their salvage work, did their bit to make it possible for General Montgomery to carry out his astounding drive against Rommel—the drive that proved to be the turning point of World War II.

Ellsberg once told me that the nearest he ever came to death was the day he went down to examine the sunken submarine *S-4*, in 1927. The *S-4* had collided with a Coast Guard destroyer off the coast of Massachusetts and had sunk in 110 feet of water. Forty men were trapped inside that submarine. The news of the disaster caused a national sensation. Although Ellsberg was no longer in the Navy then, he was one of the nation's outstanding authorities on deep-sea diving; so he volunteered his services and was rushed to the scene of the sunken submarine off Cape Cod. For three days a storm raged over the sea, making it impossible for divers to descend. By the time the storm subsided, the forty men trapped inside the submarine were dead. However, Ellsberg put on his diving suit and descended to the bottom of the ocean anyway, to see if the submarine could be lifted without breaking it in two.

Suddenly, while inspecting the submarine, Ellsberg lost all sense of direction. He knew he was still standing on the rounded hull of the sunken submarine, but he was surrounded by a cloud of mud. He couldn't see any part of the submarine itself. One step in the wrong direction might mean death. This is the story in his own words:

"I stopped instantly," he said. "I was afraid that if I took a single step the wrong way, I would go sliding overboard from the round hull on which I stood.

"I was completely lost. I stood there motionless, afraid to move.

"Then the *Falcon,* the ship to which my lifeline was fastened on the surface of the sea, took a sudden lunge on a wave and my lifeline tightened. I was thrown off balance and down I went, over the side of the sunken submarine.

167

"I was terrified because I had cut open my watertight glove and was rapidly losing air. As the air went out, the sea began pressing in on my chest. I could hardly breathe. I knew my chest would soon be crushed. I hit bottom, but instead of stopping, I shot down farther into the soft mud. I was in total darkness and I was lying on the twisted wreckage which had been torn from the keel of the ship that sunk the submarine. I feared that if I moved, those jagged steel plates would cut my suit wide open, and that would mean almost instant death.

"Finally, in desperation, I signaled my helper on the surface to pull up my lifeline. Four men heaved on the lines, but I couldn't feel the slightest pull. My lines were fouled in the wreckage above me. I could feel the pressure of the Atlantic numbing my brain. I kept thinking of the forty dead men inside the sunken submarine and I knew I would soon join them in death.

"Then gradually I became aware of a persistent murmur. I was still getting some air through my air hose. I opened wide the air inlet valve and suddenly the air started to inflate my suit. Then, as if a giant hand had seized me by the shoulders, my body started to float upward through the mud. Another moment and I was free of that bed of sharp, torn steel plates. Then my helmet burst through the ooze of the ocean floor into the water and into the light.

"I looked up. My lifeline and air hose were floating straight above me. I was clear at last. I was saved."

Every day for two and a half years, while he was attending Annapolis, Edward Ellsberg passed a flag-draped coffin which lay under the stairs in the barracks. This coffin contained the body of one of America's greatest naval heroes, Captain John Paul Jones. Edward Ellsberg became so interested in the life story of John Paul Jones that he read every book that had ever been published about him. Finally, Ellsberg himself wrote a book about John Paul Jones. He told me that his own life had been deeply influenced by the spirit of this young Scotsman who became a sailor at twelve and captain of the U. S. frigate *Ranger* at twenty-seven. Captain Ellsberg was inspired, as every American ought to be inspired, by the fighting spirit of John Paul Jones—the spirit which inspired him to answer the enemy's demand for surrender with these immortal words: "Surrender? Never. I have just begun to fight." And those words seem to have been Captain Ellsberg's life-long motto, for when anyone says to him, "It cannot be done," Edward Ellsberg just goes ahead and does it.

AMERICA'S MOST FAMOUS SONG WRITER
CAN'T READ MUSIC

AT LEAST ONE MAN is glad that he went broke in the Wall Street crash of 1929. He lost every dollar he had. One year he had millions and the next he was so broke that he had to borrow ten thousand dollars to help produce a new show. His wife told me recently that he is glad now that he went broke in 1929 because it forced him to go back to the work he loved—the work of writing songs. That man is Irving Berlin, and the first show he wrote after the 1929 crash was *As Thousands Cheer*.

In 1929 Irving Berlin knew that he had all the money he could ever use; so he was spending all his time traveling and loafing. He was having a glorious time and felt that he wanted to go on doing that forever. But he knows now that he found much more joy in again writing songs than he could ever have found in loafing.

He was worried in 1930 as to whether he could ever make the grade again. After all, he had been writing popular song hits for eighteen years and he feared that he was through, that he was written out.

But Irving Berlin had to go to work; so he wrote *As Thousands Cheer*. It was a smash hit. His confidence mounted. Hollywood asked him to write a new musical show called *Top Hat*. Hollywood wanted to pay him a flat fee, but he insisted on a percentage of the profits; and out of the five songs he wrote for that picture (one of them was "Cheek to Cheek") he made almost a third of a million dollars.

Since then he has written one hit after another—songs such

as "The Easter Parade" and "White Christmas." In 1942 he wrote and produced the most famous show of his career: *This Is the Army.* He wrote it without any compensation, giving all of his time and talent to the Government. *This Is the Army* has already made a profit of twelve million dollars, which has been given to the Army Emergency Relief Fund.

Although Irving Berlin is the world's most famous living writer of popular songs, the astonishing fact is that he knows so little about the technical aspects of music that he can't write down in musical notes the tunes that well up out of his heart. He hums the tunes while a musical secretary writes down the notes of the melody he creates.

Irving Berlin never took a music lesson in his life, yet he has probably affected the popular music of America more than any other living man. That is not my idea. That is the conviction of one of America's most distinguished composers of serious music, John Alden Carpenter. Mr. Carpenter says: "I am strongly inclined to believe that the musical historian of the year 2000 will find the birthday of American music and that of Irving Berlin to have been the same."

Irving Berlin can't even read music, yet he has written more songs than any other living man. His songs add up to more than eight hundred. He says that he has written more failures than any one else because his output has been so large.

He attended school only two years; the first book he ever read all the way through was probably the story of his own life. The biographies of most famous men are written either when they are very old, or after they are dead; Alexander Woollcott wrote a biography of Irving Berlin when Berlin was only thirty-five.

Irving Berlin made exactly thirty-three cents on the first song he wrote—"Marie from Sunny Italy"—yet three years later he wrote a song that made him a fifth of a million dollars, a song that ushered in a new era of American music, a song that made him famous overnight. It was "Alexander's Ragtime Band."

It became one of the great song hits of all time; yet it was turned down before publication by the director of a famous Broadway musical revue, the *Follies Bergere*. The director refused "Alexander's Ragtime Band" because he feared it would not be popular. But George M. Cohan knew what America liked. He grabbed the song, used it in the *Friar's Frolics* of 1911, and set a nation singing and swaying and dancing to its contagious melodies.

In 1940 the National Committee for Music Appreciation gave Irving Berlin a medal for the best composition of that year. That honor was conferred upon him for having created "God Bless America," a song that has become almost a second national anthem.

"God Bless America" was written during the first World War, but was not published until 1939. It was published after the Munich crisis because Irving Berlin feared that another war was about to devastate the world and he wanted a song to stir and unite the hearts of Americans. He feared, too, that he might be accused of making money out of patriotism; so he gave all the royalties of the song to the Girl and Boy Scouts of America.

The first time that Irving Berlin ever heard the words "God bless America" he heard them from his mother's lips. She didn't utter these words in English, for this daughter of Judah never attempted to speak the alien tongue she found here in the New World. She said "God bless America" in Russian; and she said it not casually, but with emotion bordering on exultation. She had reason to thank God for the safety and freedom of America, for she and her husband and six children had been hounded and persecuted in Russia and forced to flee for their very lives. The only memory that Irving Berlin has of his native Russia is the memory of seeing his home go up in flames in the darkness.

Irving Berlin's family sailed for America in 1892, in the hold of a crowded ship where the lights were dim and the air was

Irving Berlin

a stench. Berlin has a scar on his forehead today, caused by a knife that slipped out of the fingers of the man sleeping in the berth above him on that ship.

When this penniless family arrived in the New World, the four daughters did needlework at home, and the oldest son worked in a sweatshop. The father occasionally got a job certifying meat in kosher butcher shops, and sometimes he was paid for singing in the synagogue. The family of eight lived at first in a dark cellar, then moved into a tiny two-room flat in the slums of New York. Yet, compared to the fire and blood this Jewish mother had known in Russia, life here in the new world seemed a veritable paradise; and with a prayer of thanksgiving on her lips, she murmured over and over, "God bless America! God bless America!"

Irving Berlin himself once said: "You can't write a song out of thin air. You have to know and feel what you are writing about." He didn't have to write "God Bless America" out of thin air. He found the spirit of that song in the tales his mother taught him. He found the words of that song in the depths of his own heart.

Many of Irving Berlin's songs have developed out of his own life. When his first wife died in 1911, six months after their marriage, he wrote "When I Lost You." When, as a soldier in 1917, he groaned and agonized because he had to get out of bed at six o'clock in the morning, he wrote "Oh, How I Hate to Get Up in the Morning." When the charming Ellin Mackay fell in love with Irving Berlin and was sent to Europe by an angry father so she would forget him, he wrote "All Alone" and "Remember." Shortly before they were married, he again put his emotions into a song: "I'll Be Loving You, Always."

Mrs. Berlin once showed me a gold cigarette case that Irving had given her on her birthday. On the lid of the case was engraved the word *Always,* and the musical notes that carry the words of "I'll Be Loving You, Always." And he has been loving her all the days since they met back in the twenties. He is proud of her, and she is proud to be the wife of Irving Berlin. I could feel that as I talked to her.

The marriage of Irving Berlin and Ellin Mackay created a sensation in social circles. It was bound to end in disaster. At least that was what the wiseacres prophesied, because the bride and groom were at the opposite ends of the social scale. Her father was a leader of New York society; she had been reared in a mansion; Irving had once sung in a Bowery saloon and used the pennies that were tossed to him in the sawdust to pay for a bed in a cheap lodging house.

But in spite of all the dire warnings, their marriage has vibrated with happiness. It has helped to break down false social distinctions. They have three daughters, and they spend their summers quietly on a fifty-two-acre farm in the Catskill Mountains. Mr. and Mrs. Irving Berlin don't care for night clubs or society. Their work is their life.

As I have already said, Irving Berlin never took a music lesson in his life, but he did learn early in his career something that he could not and would not have been taught in the finest conservatory of music. He learned how to compose the verses and create the tunes that the common people like. He learned it by leading a blind musician from corner to corner on the Bowery and by singing the tunes that the blind musician played. He also learned it by singing in Bowery saloons and restaurants and theaters. He sometimes sang new words to the old music— words that he himself had composed—and watched the effect on his listeners.

Later he composed his own tunes and tried them on crowds in restaurants and beer halls. He composed and sang his melodies to the tempo of America. His music was influenced not by the classics of the Old World, but by the heartbeat of the New World.

Few men ever crowded more living into their lives, and few men have ever found such beautiful melodies in the depths of their hearts.

THE ONLY MAN IN HISTORY WHO WAS EVER ATTACKED BY BOWS AND ARROWS AS WELL AS DIVE-BOMBERS

ONLY ONE GENERAL in the United States Army has been attacked by bows and arrows, as well as by airplanes and bombs. Who do you suppose that general is?

Well, I am speaking about General Douglas MacArthur, Chief of Operations in the Southwest Pacific. General MacArthur has heard the zing of Indian arrows, as well as the screech of Jap dive-bombers.

After the close of the Civil War, General MacArthur's father, a Colonel in the regular Army, was stationed in the vast territory now incorporated in the state of New Mexico. Those were the wild and turbulent days of Billy the Kid and Wild Bill Hickok, the days of Custer's Massacre. MacArthur's father and his soldiers were stationed there to establish law and order.

One day in 1884 the Indians attacked the adobe compound which served as the fort. Little Douglas MacArthur was only four years old then; he escaped from the friendly Indian squaw who was paid to look after him, and ran out into the stockade where an Indian arrow missed his head by inches.

General MacArthur's earliest memory is the sound of bugles. As a boy he didn't listen to fairy stories. He listened to the sounds of guns, and to warriors telling of the heroic charges at Gettysburg and Missionary Ridge.

Young Douglas MacArthur often gazed with wonder and ad-

175

miration at the Congressional Medal of Honor his father had won during the Civil War—the highest honor a military man can win in America—and he vowed over and over that someday he, too, would win the Congressional Medal of Honor, just as his father had done. And he did! He won it half a century later for the heroic stand on Bataan and Corregidor. His forces on Bataan were outnumbered ten to one; the Japs controlled sea and air; yet MacArthur on Bataan wrote in blood and fire one of the most inspiring pages in American history.

General MacArthur isn't the back-slapping sort of individual. His friends admire him intensely, but few of them call him by his first name. Even his wife calls him "General."

Colonel Allan Pope, a classmate of MacArthur at West Point, knows the General intimately. He told me that MacArthur was a formal man, a "gentleman of the old school," with a flair for colorful language and a dramatic way of talking. Colonel Pope told me that General MacArthur clips off his words, enunciates each syllable clearly.

General MacArthur is a great soldier and fighter, yet he is very sentimental. When they were cadets together in West Point, Pope and MacArthur went to see David Warfield in *The Music Master,* and MacArthur was so carried away that he wept over the play.

When MacArthur went out to the Philippines, the blinding heat and boredom tempted him at times to go in for the easy life of drinking and dancing that many of the other young officers led. But when he was tempted to do that, he would stand before a full-length mirror and lecture himself with all the fervor of a top-sergeant bawling out a private.

General MacArthur graduated with the highest marks anyone had made at West Point in a quarter of a century—the top man in his class. His classmates felt he was destined to be a leader. Fortune has always smiled on him. Let me read you his record.

General Douglas MacArthur was the youngest man to hold the rank of major general; he was the first American to be made a four-star general twice. He was the youngest man ever to serve as Superintendent of West Point.

MacArthur has won more American decorations than were ever given any other Army officer, plus medals from ten foreign governments. He was the first American Army officer ever to become a field marshal—an honor conferred upon him by the Philippine Government. He was the first American to take complete command of the land, sea, and air forces of Allied nations.

He was the youngest full general since Grant and the first ever to be awarded the Congressional Medal of Honor. As military advisor to the Philippine Commonwealth, he probably was paid the highest salary ever paid to any military advisor in the world. MacArthur was the youngest Chief of Staff of the United States Army, and he was the first Chief of Staff ever to be reappointed at the end of his four-year term.

Has any other man in American military history piled up a similar record? I doubt it.

General MacArthur was ill with a high fever the day the great American attack was launched against Saint-Mihiel in France, during the first World War. But, fever or no fever, MacArthur was determined to direct the 84th Brigade in that attack. He was so weak he feared he would be unable to walk to the front; so he told four orderlies that if he couldn't walk they must carry him to the front that morning on a stretcher. The late General Hugh Johnson, a sour and hard-hitting critic, said: "MacArthur is one general who will not die in bed if there is half a chance to die elsewhere."

In the first World War there was no holding MacArthur when he got out where the shells were bursting. He created a sensation by going into battle himself with his own men. He was cited for bravery because he helped his men capture a machine-gun nest. The citation read: "On a field where courage was the rule, his courage was the dominant feature."

During the first World War, he was gassed, wounded twice,

177

decorated thirteen times for "extreme bravery under fire," and cited seven additional times for bravery. It is not surprising that Newton D. Baker, Secretary of War in 1918, called Mac-Arthur America's greatest front-line fighting general in the first World War.

When MacArthur was out on raiding parties with his men in those days, he carried no gun, no sword, no revolver—nothing but a riding whip. His men called him "a hell-to-breakfast baby." He felt his show of courage would inspire his men to be courageous. General MacArthur feels that it is up to him to set an example. If he expects his men to be courageous, he knows that he himself must express confidence and courage. That is why he refused to take down the American flag that flew over his headquarters in Manila. He refused to lower the flag even when the Japs were bombing the city. To be sure, the flag made a great target for the Jap bombing planes overhead, but Mac-Arthur kept on working calmly, inside the building, dictating reports, sending cables, telephoning orders. He felt it would hurt the morale of his men if he lowered the flag or left the building for a safer place.

General MacArthur has repeatedly said: "Only those are fit to live who are not afraid to die."

MacArthur has the ability to inspire his men and to send them into battle with his own contagious zeal and enthusiasm. The men under MacArthur know and feel that they are fighting for their homes and families and freedom.

Colonel Carlos Romulo is the author of a book entitled *I Saw the Fall of the Philippines.* He was also personal aide to General MacArthur on Bataan and Corregidor. I interviewed him recently, and he told me that MacArthur refused to wear a tin helmet during the battle of Bataan. He insisted that his men wear them, but he felt he could best inspire courage in the men by not wearing one himself. One day while shrapnel was falling, MacArthur's orderly took off his own helmet and tried to

178

put it on MacArthur's head. MacArthur pushed it away; as he did so, a bit of shrapnel pierced the orderly's hand. Colonel Romulo also told me that one day on Bataan General Mac-Arthur was sitting in a garden when the Jap dive-bombers appeared overhead. He started walking calmly to the bomb shelter, when a friend urged him to hurry. MacArthur serenely lighted a cigarette and said, "There isn't a Jap living who can make me hurry."

When Colonel Carlos Romulo asked the Philippine soldiers on Bataan what they were fighting for, they didn't say a word about America. They said they were fighting for MacArthur and President Quezon of the Philippines. To the Filipinos, MacArthur is America. In peace times even the lowliest citizen could get an interview with MacArthur. Perhaps it was some barefooted worker from the rice fields who was worried about his son in the Army. MacArthur would stand up to greet the man when he came in, and he would walk to the door with him when he left. The Filipinos admired a general who would receive a barefooted worker from the rice paddies like that.

Colonel Romulo told me that he had often seen MacArthur on Bataan calling privates by their first names and smiling as he returned their salutes.

As Chief of Staff of the Army, MacArthur demonstrated that he has outstanding ability as an administrator; he also demonstrated that he has vision and foresight. He prophesied years ago that World War II was coming soon and that it would be vastly different from the first World War. He prophesied years ago that this war would be fought with the speed of tanks racing across the country at a mile a minute, with the speed of airplanes shooting through the sky at four hundred miles an hour. He cried over and over again that Japan and Germany were preparing to conquer the world.

If we had only listened to MacArthur and given the money he pleaded for to build a mechanized army, Japan might never have attacked us at Pearl Harbor. Did we thank General MacArthur for these grave warnings? No, we denounced him as an alarmist, a war monger.

General MacArthur has only one framed motto hanging on the walls of his headquarters in Australia. It is a statement made by Abraham Lincoln to his friends who were urging him to answer his critics during the Civil War. That motto is:

"If I were to try to read, much less to answer, all the attacks made on me, this shop might as well be closed for any other business. I do the very best I know how—the very best I can; and I mean to keep on doing so until the end. If the end brings me out all right, then what is said against me won't matter. If the end brings me out wrong, then ten angels swearing I was right would make no difference."

SHE HAS TOLD A MILLION GIRLS HOW
TO GET HUSBANDS

Who would you say is the most widely read woman writer in the world? She is one of the happiest women in America because she has probably done more to help Tom, Dick, and Harriet solve their emotional problems than have all the psychologists living in the world today. For years she has been mother-confessor to millions of perplexed men and women. Probably no other living person has prevented as many divorces, saved as many homes.

The name of this remarkable woman is Mrs. Elizabeth Meriwether Gilmer. Never heard of her? Oh, yes, you have. You have heard of her many times. But you have heard of her as "Dorothy Dix." When Mrs. Gilmer started her writing career back in 1896, she took the name "Dorothy" because she liked it and she chose "Dix" in memory of a Negro servant who had once been a slave in the family. "Dorothy Dix" is the name Mrs. Gilmer signs to her daily newspaper articles that are syndicated in some two hundred papers. Her newspaper column reaches literally millions of readers scattered all the way from London to Australia and from New York to South America and South Africa.

I had the privilege some time ago of having tea with Dorothy Dix in New Orleans. She told me of her childhood, of how she was brought up in the decade that followed the Civil War on her father's big race-horse farm, situated on the border between

Tennessee and Kentucky. Dorothy Dix came from a fine old Southern family that had lost its fortunes during the Civil War. "We lived," she says, "in a curious mingling of poverty and luxury. We had a fine old house and rich lands where cattle and sheep thrived and corn and cotton grew luxuriously. We dined on a mahogany table and ate out of silver dishes. Yet we had little money."

As a child, Dorothy Dix wore linsey frocks made from the wool of her father's sheep that had been woven into cloth at a neighboring mill. She says that her nurse was a race horse, a Kentucky mare—once the pride and joy of her father's racing stable—that had grown old and stiff and was left to graze at will in the big front yard. "I learned to ride this horse before I learned to walk," Dorothy Dix said. "My father would put me on the old mare's back and I would cling to her mane as she ate the blue grass. Occasionally the mare would walk under a clothes line or the limb of a tree that would rake me off her back. I would tumble to the ground and cry until someone picked me up and put me on the horse's back again."

A Negro mammy taught manners to little Dorothy Dix and her brother and sister. She stood behind their chairs as they ate, watching them like a sentinel. If they deviated from the code of good manners, if they were greedy or picked up food with their fingers, or whined—whang! Down came the bony knuckles on their heads and Mammy would say, "Mind your manners! Don't act like poor white trash!"

Dorothy Dix and her brother and sister had only the toys that they themselves made, and they had to create their own amusements. Yet their childhood was glorious. Her childhood companions were dogs and horses and the other two children in the family. "We were free as air, there on my father's farm," she said. "No one told us where to go or what to do. We put bridles on the horses and dashed at breakneck speed through the woods, with the dogs yelping and barking behind us. We

Dorothy Dix

knew all the secrets of the woods. We knew where the quail hid, where the hawks built their nests, and where the rabbits reared their young. We knew where the wild plums grew and where the best hickory nuts were to be found in the autumn. We soon developed self-confidence and self-reliance, for we were thrown on our own resources, and if we got into trouble we had to get out of it ourselves. We were taught to keep God's commandments, to tell the truth always, and that gentlefolk do not whine."

And here is one of the strangest facts I know about Dorothy Dix: She got the most valuable part of her education from an old man who was half-demented. He had once been a good friend of her grandfather; so he lived without cost in the home in which she was reared. This old man taught Dorothy Dix not only to read, but also to love the good books in her father's library. "Before I was twelve," Dorothy Dix says, "I knew my Shakespeare and Scott and Dickens by heart and had read Smollett and Fielding and Richardson—had even toyed with the works of Josephus, with Motley's *Dutch Republic,* and with other airy literary trifles like that.

"I had no children's books to read, and so I cut my teeth on the solid meat of good literature. I have always been very glad that I did."

Dorothy Dix got very little formal schooling. She said: "I was sent to school to Miss Alice's or Miss Jenny's, not because they were qualified to teach, but because their fathers had been colonels under Beauregard or had been killed at Gettysburg and somebody had to help the poor souls make a living." Dorothy Dix could climb trees like a squirrel and could ride like a jockey before she knew that seven times seven is forty-nine. Whatever real education she got, she dug out of the yellow old books in her father's library.

"When I was eighteen," Dorothy Dix says, "I tucked up my hair and got married, as was the tribal custom among my

183

people." She expected to lead the kind of a life that thousands of other girls in her circumstances led. But tragedy struck her straight between the eyes and overwhelmed her with domestic and financial disaster. Her husband soon became a hopeless invalid. She had to nurse and support him until his death thirty-five years later. She didn't know how she could make a dollar. She didn't know how she could support even herself, let alone an invalid husband. She suffered so much mental agony that she grew ill and had to be sent down to the Gulf Coast of Mississippi to get well.

That trip to the Gulf Coast revolutionized her life. While resting at the seashore, Dorothy Dix wrote a little story founded on an incident that had happened in her family during the Civil War. The family feared that the silver might be stolen by marauding bands of Yankee soldiers; so a family slave hid the precious silver among the cast-iron caskets in the family tomb. The slave not only hid the silver; he also ordered the ghosts in the graveyard to watch over it and keep the thieves away. Dorothy Dix sold the story she wrote about that incident to a woman who happened to be living next door to her down on the Gulf Coast. This woman owned one of the most famous newspapers in the South, the New Orleans *Picayune*. She paid Dorothy Dix three dollars for the story and then hired her to work as a reporter on the *Picayune*. That job paid only five dollars a week, and on that five dollars she had to support herself and her invalid husband. That job launched Dorothy Dix on a career that has made her name a household word and herself an American institution.

One of Dorothy Dix's first assignments was to write a Sunday feature article for women entitled "Sunday Salad"—an article of advice to women on how to manage their emotions, their children, and their husbands. She refused to use the highfalutin' literary language that most women writers used in that day. She wrote just as she talked—and women loved it.

184

Dorothy Dix

Her articles caught on. William Randolph Hearst, who was always looking for new talent, offered her a tremendous increase in salary to join his *Evening Journal* in New York. She needed the extra money, but she refused to leave her old employer. The New Orleans *Picayune* had taught her almost everything she knew about newspaper work. The editor was ill now and depending on her. She refused to leave. But after that editor's death in 1901, she did join the Hearst organization in New York; and, for the next twenty years, she not only wrote her advice to the lovelorn, but she became the original sobsister—that is, she reported, from a human-interest standpoint, all the sensational news, such as the big murder trials. She covered the trial of Harry K. Thaw, the Pittsburgh millionaire who shot Stanford White, New York's most famous architect, on the crowded roof of famous old Madison Square Garden; the sensational trial of Nan Patterson, a member of the original Floradora Sextette; the trial of Ruth Snyder and Judd Gray; the trial of Lefty Louie, Gyp the Blood, and Police Captain Becker; and the Hall-Mills case, one of the most sensational murder mysteries of the twentieth century.

The little unsophisticated girl who, until she was twenty, had not ridden on a train more than half a dozen times; who, until she was twenty, had never seen a real play in a theater or been to a city more than twice—this little unsophisticated girl from an isolated Kentucky farm had now become the most famous woman journalist in New York.

Dorothy Dix is often asked whether or not she makes up the letters which she answers in her column. The answer most emphatically is "no," because she gets from a hundred to a thousand real letters every day. She declares that those letters are the most amazing human documents—a cross-section of life, raw and bleeding life—with nothing covered up and nothing hidden. She says the letters give her an insight to the human heart such as probably no other person has ever been granted.

185

She is asked the most incredible questions—whether or not it is bad luck to have a baby on Friday, how to go to bed in a Pullman car, how to play volleyball, how to eat a stuffed tomato, what to name an Airedale dog. Here are two typical extracts from her letters:

"Miss Dix, I know you have traveled a great deal, so I want you to tell me if there is such a thing as really truly a cure for superfluous hair."

"Miss Dix, why am I not able to attract men? I have a medium-sized nose, full lips, and a college education."

Dorothy Dix has had honorary degrees bestowed upon her by Tulane and Oglethorpe Universities; but she declares that the title that goes straight to her heart is the one given her when some bewildered, troubled girl or boy begins a letter to her, a woman who has never had any children of her own, with these words: "My more-than-mother, I know you will understand . . ."

HE COMMANDED HIS ITALIANS TO "LIVE DANGEROUSLY"—BUT HE WAS AFRAID TO GO HOME IN THE DARK

SHORTLY AFTER THE TURN of the century a man was out of work in Switzerland. He had heard wonderful stories of how easy it was to make money in America. So one day he tossed a coin into the air. If heads came up, he would go to America. If tails, he would stay in Switzerland. Tails came up—and changed history. If that man had gone to America, Italy would probably not have been plunged into the second World War, for the man who tossed that coin into the air was Benito Mussolini. If Mussolini had come to America, he might have become another Al Capone, but he certainly would never have become Dictator of Italy, and the chances are that under those conditions Italy never would have formed an alliance with Hitler. In fact, if Mussolini had not become Dictator of Italy, Hitler might never have become powerful. Hitler was a nobody when Mussolini first grabbed dictatorial powers; from Mussolini Hitler learned how to seize power and become a dictator.

But to come back to my story. In 1904 Mussolini had fled from Italy to Switzerland on a faked passport to avoid being conscripted into the army. He got a job as a porter in a railway station, carrying suitcases and accepting tips. He also worked as a bricklayer and as a delivery boy for a butcher shop. But he was always quarreling with people, always getting fired. He was often dead broke and frequently slept on the ground under

187

bridges. His clothes were ragged and filthy. He got so hungry sometimes that he begged for money on the street. Once he stole bread from two women picnicking in the park. Another time he stole a gold watch. The police arrested Benito Mussolini and threw him into jail eleven times.

When Mussolini was a child, he had no bed to sleep on; he slept on a pile of straw like a dog. He was brought up in an atmosphere of poverty and hate. His father, who was first a blacksmith and then a saloonkeeper, hated the rich, the Government, and the Church. He was sent to prison for three years for his revolutionary activities and he named his son after Benito Juarez, one of the wildest revolutionists in Mexican history—the man who kicked the Emperor Maximilian off the throne of Mexico and had him shot.

Mussolini spent his childhood in that atmosphere of hate and rebellion. "I was a country thief," he said, "always ready to fight. I often came home with my head broken with stones, but I knew how to get revenge."

Mussolini, like Hitler, tried to compensate for his bitter youth by seizing power and glory. As a boy, he sought power and glory by fighting other boys, but he was always careful to jump on boys smaller than himself—boys he knew he could easily whip. Forty years later he got revenge by picking on smaller nations that he knew had no chance to defend themselves against Italy—nations like Ethopia and Albania.

All his life Mussolini used the sneak attack. Once when another boy slapped him, Mussolini got a sharp rock, hid behind some bushes, leaped on the back of the boy as he passed and cut his face open with the rock. Even after Mussolini became Dictator of Italy, he used to brag about this fight. He was so wild and fierce that his mother sent him to a Church school, hoping that the Catholic Friars might soften her son. But even in the Church school he stabbed another boy in the back with a knife, just as forty years later he stabbed fallen and bleeding

188

France in the back. The Friars expelled Benito Mussolini from their school saying, "Your soul is black as hell."

Did Mussolini blame himself for all his troubles? No, of course not. He blamed everybody except himself. Years later, he said: "No one has ever shown me any tenderness. As a child, I lived in a poor home and my life was bitter. Where could I have learned tenderness? Nowhere. Then why do people wonder that I am harsh and stern?"

Wherever Mussolini went, he expressed hate and violence. For example, in Zurich he once thought that a waitress had charged him twenty-five cents too much; he became so enraged that he and three other Italians turned over the tables, smashed the chairs, and wrecked the place.

Mussolini, the man who ordered the Italians to "live dangerously," was such a coward that when he was editor of the Socialist paper, *Avanti,* he always kept a long knife and loaded revolver on his desk. His assistant editor, a woman, probably knew him better than anyone else on earth at that period, and she said she was astonished at his "incredible physical fear." Mussolini confessed to her that he was afraid even of his own shadow. He was such a coward that he was afraid to go home in the dark. He was ashamed to admit this to the men in his office; so he asked his woman assistant to see him home every night. She took him to his door and then went on alone to her own house.

I am not reporting mere hearsay or gossip. The woman who took the frightened Caesar home every night told this story herself in print. Her name is Angelica Balabanoff and for many years she was one of the most brilliant and famous leaders of the Socialist Party—a woman whose integrity is above question.

After he became Dictator of Italy, seven attempts were made to assassinate Mussolini. He became so alarmed that he had a private army of fifteen thousand soldiers guarding every foot of his home and office day and night.

Biographical Roundup

For years, ulcers gnawed at Mussolini's stomach—ulcers that were probably produced by worries and fears for his own safety.

Although Mussolini never learned to read until he was fifteen, he devoured many books as he grew older. However, in many ways he remained incredibly ignorant and superstitious. For example, he believes that the moon has a profound effect upon human destiny. Yes, this bombastic Mussolini who shouted to the Italians to "live dangerously" is afraid to sleep with the moon shining on his face, and he believes that he can interpret dreams and forecast the future by looking at a deck of cards. Before Mussolini made his historic march on Rome to seize the Government, he laid a deck of cards out on the table and studied them carefully—not once, but many times.

How do we know all this is true? We know it because it was recorded in Mussolini's official biography—a biography that he himself read, approved, and wrote an introduction for.

Mussolini is a profound neurotic. For years he suffered from half-insane delusions of grandeur. In every insane asylum you will always find some poor fellow who imagines he is Napoleon. Mussolini never quite believed he was an original Julius Caesar, but he did believe he was a second Julius Caesar. He ordered sculptors to make busts of himself looking like Caesar; when he visited Tripoli in 1926, he authorized throughout the colony thousands of colored posters that welcomed him with the words, "Hail, Caesar!"

Mussolini himself declared: "I want to make my mark in history with my Will. I want to make a mark such as a lion makes with his claws. I am obsessed with this wild desire. It consumes my whole being."

Those four sentences explain Mussolini's entire life. They are the confessions of an insane egotist, the confessions of a man who sent half a million men to bloody deaths on the battlefield so that he could be glorified in history as the twentieth-century Julius Caesar.

190

HE HAS THE BUMPS IN HIS THROAT INSURED FOR ONE HUNDRED THOUSAND DOLLARS

WHO WOULD YOU NAME as the highest-priced singer this world has ever known? Caruso? Melchior? Tibbett? Well, guess again—for the highest-paid singer of all time is a man who never took a music lesson in his life, and who owes his voice to an accident of nature, to a freak formation of his vocal chords.

He's Harry Lillis Crosby—"Bing" to you—and in one year this happy-go-lucky crooner, who's always caroling: "I'm no millionaire, but I'm not the type to care," earned just a little better than three-quarters of a million dollars. Yes, in 1943 Bing Crosby made seven times as much money as did Franklin D. Roosevelt and Winston Churchill together. And that, if you ask me, is a pretty good stack of "pennies from heaven."

The career of this "groaner"—for that's what he calls himself —is one of the most astonishing success stories of the twentieth century. Bing was born in 1904. He's lost so much hair that he has to wear a toupee. His ears stick out so far they have to be taped back to his head when he's making a picture. He chews a wad of gum even during love scenes, and yet he's the romantic idol of millions of women and the undisputed favorite of millions of men. When General MacArthur was trapped in the Philippines and Roosevelt asked what the American troops would like to help boost their morale, MacArthur radioed the White House that his men on Bataan wanted Bing Crosby. Yes, even at a time like that, they wanted to hear that old familiar

191

voice crooning: "When the blue of the night meets the gold of the day."

Not only that, but six thousand years from now your descendants may be gathered around the victrola of the future, listening to Bing Crosby's dulcet tones warbling out of the past. For, some years ago, when Dr. Thornwell Jacobs of Oglethorpe University was asked to choose the objects to be sealed in the Time Vault—the Time Vault that isn't to be opened till the eighty-first century—he included one of Bing Crosby's records. The reason? Nothing, he said, could be more representative of our present era; for not a second passes on this spinning earth that Bing Crosby's songs aren't being played by somebody, somewhere, twenty-four hours a day.

Incredible, isn't it? And what do you suppose is the secret of this phenomenal voice? Well, according to the doctors, it's all due to a series of little bumps inside of Bing's throat. Sometime ago a surgeon offered to remove these bumps by operation. But Bing said: "No sir! That's why I sound as though I were singin' down a rain-barrel!" And today those bumps are insured for a hundred thousand dollars.

Some people have described Bing Crosby as the laziest living man, who owes everything to luck and who never had to struggle a day for success. Well, judge for yourself. When he was a boy back home in Spokane, he spent all his vacations (when other kids were playing) working in a pickle factory. When he wasn't wrestling pickles, he was delivering papers, or pitching hay on a farm, or even stoking up fires in a lumber camp. And in 1931, when he got his first break as a singer, he filled the unbelievable schedule of appearing five times daily at the Paramount Theatre here in New York, dashing between shows to the radio studios for two programs nightly, and making victrola records in addition to that. So even if he says, "I'm just a very lucky guy," you can see for yourself it wasn't all done with mirrors.

Bing Crosby

If you ask Bing Crosby what he considers the single greatest asset that has contributed to his success, he'll tell you it was a course he took in speaking in college. That speaking course taught him diction and phrasing—and, as he puts it, "If I'm not a singer, I am a phraser. I owe it all to that training."

Bing Crosby is the romantic idol of millions of women, yet when he first proposed to his wife, Dixie Lee, she turned him down flat. Bing, she said, was nothing but a playboy who seemed to regard the whole United States as a patch in which to sow his wild oats; who thought it was a lark to land in jail; and who spent so much money that somebody warned her, "If you marry Bing Crosby, you'll have to support him for life!"

That was the kick in the teeth that woke Bing up. Almost overnight he handed over all his financial affairs to his father and his brothers and settled down to become a family man who went to church every Sunday. Today he and Dixie Lee have four strapping sons, and the firm of Bing Crosby, Ltd., Inc. (yes, that's what it's called!) has spread out until it has been described as "a minor business octopus." Bing gets twenty-five dollars a week to spend for chewing-gum and tobacco, and the rest of his money goes into the firm. With it, his father and brothers have invested in real estate, gold mines, office buildings, and oil wells.

Every day in the week Bing gets up at seven to start his day at the studios; but he rarely goes near his office, except to take a bath. It seems there are some Finnish baths on the ground floor of the Crosby Building, and Bing has discovered he can dope out the race-sheets while he lies around and soaks.

He loves to swim; and in order to win a bet during the World's Fair in New York, he made a high-dive of fifty feet, to the astonishment of the audience. He loves golf so much that he sometimes gets up at five in the morning to play a few holes; Gene Sarazen says that if Bing tried hard enough, he might be another Bobby Jones.

X

Biographical Roundup

Yes, there are very few things this lazy-looking guy of the loud sweaters can't do—including writing. He's got a batch of short stories tucked away in a trunk, and some day he hopes to hit the bigger magazines. He often rewrites his radio scripts, and even his pictures.

But there's one thing this box-office star who has made more than thirty pictures, insists he can't do. A reporter once asked him, "Tell me, Mr. Crosby, which one of your pictures first convinced Paramount you were able to act?" And Bing answered with a grin, "You've got me there, Mister. This is the first I've heard that they'd made up their minds!"

HE WAS ON HIS WAY TO THE GRAVEYARD TO BE BURIED IN WORLD WAR I; YET HE BECAME GREAT BRITAIN'S MOST FAMOUS GENERAL IN WORLD WAR II

NINE HUNDRED AND TWO WARS have been fought in the past 2500 years, and yet the British general, Sir Bernard Montgomery, has established a new record in the art of war. He waged a campaign that has never been equaled before in all the annals of recorded history. He and his Eighth Army, "the Army of the Nile," chased General Rommel and his *Afrika Korps* fifteen hundred miles across the African desert in fifteen weeks. That's equal to half the distance across the American Continent, from the Atlantic Ocean to Denver, Colorado.

Before the campaign started, General Montgomery told his soldiers that they were going to fight one of the decisive battles of history—a battle that would prove to be a turning point of this war. And it was just that. If General Montgomery had met defeat and disaster at El Alamein, the Germans would have taken Egypt, the Suez Canal, and probably the oil wells of Iran and Iraq. They might then have swept on through India, joined hands with the Japs, and cut off all supplies from Russia and China. Yes, General Montgomery was certainly right when he told his troops at El Alamein that they were fighting one of the decisive battles of history.

Yet General Montgomery came very near to not fighting the

195

Y

battle of El Alamein at all. For in the first World War, he was so seriously wounded in the lung during the battle of Meteron that he was on his way to the grave, about to be buried alive. His own mother has told the story much better than I could:

"Bernard fell," she writes, "and his orderly, who was shot through the heart, dropped dead on top of him. Bernard lost consciousness and was carried to a clearing station, where the doctor said, 'This man has only half an hour to live.' The colonel ordered a grave to be dug. Bernard was put on a lorry. On the way to the burial, the driver thought he saw a slight movement. So he yelled to the doctor, 'That corpse isn't dead, sir!' "

Yes, thank God, that corpse wasn't dead, for that corpse is now regarded as one of the most brilliant British Generals brought into the limelight by World War II.

General Sir Bernard Law Montgomery, "Monty of El Alamein," came very nearly being a preacher instead of a general. He is not really English. True, he was born in London, but he is Irish, both on his mother's side and his father's side. His father was the Right Reverend H. H. Montgomery, the Bishop of Tasmania in the Episcopalian Church, and Bernard Montgomery, as a child, expected to follow in the footsteps of his father.

But in 1899, when Bernard was twelve years old, he stood on the sidewalks of London, watching the soldiers marching away to the Boer War. Bands filled the air with stirring martial music. The streets overflowed with excited crowds shouting and cheering. As he stood there, little Bernard Montgomery thought of the tales of adventure that his mother had read to him as a child, tales of how his own grandfather, Sir Robert Montgomery, had become Lieutenant-General of the Punjab and achieved fame in the Indian Mutiny. Then and there, this twelve-year-old boy resolved, with a surge of emotion, that he, too, would become, not a bishop, but a great military leader like his grandfather. He, too, would march through the streets of London some day, with flags waving and crowds cheering.

General Montgomery's mother fostered in him a spirit of adventure by reading to him the lives of Cromwell, Clive, Lord Nelson, and Drake—famous men in English history.

He was reared in a home filled with immortal books and inspiring thoughts and ideals. One day his father called his four sons into the library and told them they were old enough to choose their own paths in life. He didn't try to tell them what to do, but he did say that regardless of what paths they chose, he hoped they would all serve the Empire.

As part of his preparation to serve the Empire, General Montgomery graduated from the Royal Military College at Sandhurst, the West Point of England. He has spent the last thirty-seven years as a professional army officer.

Much of his outstanding military success has been due to his ability to lead and inspire men. He declares that the first essential for success in war is the human factor. "It is not the tank, the armored car, or the battleship that is going to win the war," he says. "It is the men inside them."

He declares that "every man in the army must have the light of battle in his eye." He told his Eighth Army that they were the best soldiers on this planet, that they had covered themselves with glory, that they never had failed to beat the enemy, and that no power on earth could stop them. He also took them into his confidence and told them precisely what they were going to do. He gave them definite objectives. He assured them that he would never send them into battle unless they had the equipment and ammunition and air power necessary to achieve victory. General Montgomery told his troops that he had two rules for combat:

First, never allow yourself to be rushed.

Second, never undertake a campaign unless you are certain

you will be successful. "I never fight battles," he once said in a message to his troops, "unless I know I can win. If I am worried about a battle, I don't fight it.' I wait until I get ready."

General Montgomery isn't merely a soldier. He is a hawk-eyed crusader in khaki, a Billy Sunday in a tank. Soldiering to him isn't a profession. It is an obsession. He loves the excitement of battle and is profoundly convinced that he is fighting at Armageddon and battling for the Lord. You will find two books at his headquarters on the battlefield—John Bunyan's *Pilgrim's Progress* and the Bible. He recommends that all his officers read the Bible. His hero is Oliver Cromwell; so he was immensely pleased when Winston Churchill compared him to Cromwell. One can almost imagine General Montgomery going into battle singing hymns as did the troops of Cromwell.

Like Generals Eisenhower, MacArthur, and many of the other top-ranking allied leaders, General Montgomery is a deeply religious man. He never drinks, never swears, never smokes, prays each night, and gives one-tenth of his income to the church.

He is a strict disciplinarian, too. He once issued an order at a military conference, saying, "I do not approve of smoking or coughing. There will be no smoking. You may cough now for two minutes. Thereafter coughing will cease for twenty minutes, when I shall allow another sixty seconds for coughing."

General Montgomery has no personal hate for his enemies. He used to keep a picture of Rommel hanging above his bed. He repeatedly said that he wished that he had met Rommel before the war. Why? Because he feels that after he has talked to a man he is going to fight, he is in a far better position to figure out what kind of a campaign that man will wage.

When Montgomery captured Rommel's right-hand man, General Von Thoma, he invited Von Thoma to be his guest at dinner. He drew a plan of his campaign on the tablecloth and showed Von Thoma why Rommel couldn't win.

198

General Montgomery

When Montgomery commanded the Twelfth Corps, he had a sign on his office wall which read: "Are you 100 per cent fit? Are you full of vim? Do you get up in the morning with a glad shout on your lips?"

The truth of the matter is that General Montgomery himself doesn't get up with a glad shout on his lips—or any other kind of a shout, for that matter. He doesn't even get out of bed at all for an hour after he is called. He is called promptly at six in the morning, has a cup of tea in bed, and then lies there for an hour thinking and planning. He leaves details to others and organizes his day so that he never has to rush. Even on the day preceding a battle, he usually takes things easy. His battle plans have already been made. He declares that battles can and should be won before a shot is fired, won by careful planning in advance.

After a battle really starts, General Montgomery relaxes. He went to bed one hour before the great artillery barrage opened his campaign against Rommel at El Alamein. Four and a half hours later, at one-thirty in the morning, his aide awoke him to make a report. Montgomery listened, issued an order, blew out his lamp, and went back to sleep. His supreme confidence was built on his careful planning, his command of the air, his superb soldiers, and his splendid equipment.

General Montgomery didn't marry until he was forty. He has a son, David, who is fifteen. His wife died in 1937. He was so broken up by her death that for a year he saw few of his old friends. Outside of his son, he has few interests in life now, except soldiering and keeping canaries. Throughout the Italian campaign, he carried a cage of canaries and lovebirds with him in his office, which was mounted on a huge truck.

He finds time, even while fighting battles, to write to his mother, who is seventy-nine. She knitted him a pair of gloves to keep his hands warm when he crossed the English Channel to invade Germany. She remarked to a newspaper reporter, "I do hope Bernard will wear these gloves and not go and lose them."

General Montgomery has taken as his motto some words of advice that his father gave to his four sons—words in the great tradition: "You come," he said, "from a family of gentlemen. This does not signify mere outward refinement. It speaks of a refined and noble mind, to which anything dishonorable, mean, or impure, is unworthy and abhorrent."

HE ATTENDED SCHOOL ONLY SEVEN YEARS; YET HE HELD DEGREES FROM SIX UNIVERSITIES

FIFTY-EIGHT YEARS AGO an Irish truck driver died in New York City. He had been ill for a long time before his death, and had been forced to give up driving a truck and to get a job as a night watchman. When he died, he was so poor that his friends had to chip in and pay for the coffin in which he was buried. He left a widow and two children. His widow, full of visions and dreams, resolved to keep her children in school as long as she could. She got a job working in an umbrella factory ten hours a day. Her wages, however, were so small that she had to take material home from the factory and continue her work until ten or eleven o'clock at night. This mother slaved fourteen or fifteen hours a day for her children.

What a pity she wasn't able to raise the curtain of the future and to foresee that one day her little boy would be governor of the state of New York, not just once, but for four terms—longer than any other man had held the office up to that time.

What a pity this mother couldn't foresee that in 1928 her son would be the Democratic candidate for President. What a pity she couldn't know then that on May 5, 1944, the New York *Times* would call her son "the best-loved citizen of New York."

For Al Smith was just that—the favorite son of the greatest city in the Western World. And, symbolically perhaps, he was the president of the corporation that built and operated the Empire State Building, the tallest structure ever erected by man.

Biographical Roundup

I once asked Al Smith how many years he attended school. He hesitated for a while and said, "Well, let me see—let me see. . . . I don't remember exactly. I was born in 1873—oh, I guess I spent about seven or eight years in school, but I couldn't prove it. I never graduated from anything and I don't have any papers to show that I ever attended school at all."

Well, Alfred Emmanuel Smith may not have had papers to show that he ever attended school, but he did have papers to show that he had had honorary degrees conferred upon him by six great universities, including Columbia and Harvard, for his outstanding achievements in statesmanship and his unselfish devotion to humanity.

I asked Al Smith if he was sorry he didn't go to college, and he said no, he was glad of it. He declared that if a man wanted to get ahead in politics, he must have the ability to win friends and deal with human nature, and he felt that he had probably learned more about dealing with human nature while working in the Fulton Street Fish Market and while acting as a process-server for eight years than he would have learned in college.

When Alfred Emmanuel Smith was ten years old, he was an altar boy, getting out of bed at five o'clock on cold winter mornings in order to serve at the six-o'clock mass.

At the age of twelve he was a newsboy along the waterfront. In his spare time he played baseball directly under the Brooklyn Bridge, a bridge that he watched being built. But the biggest thrill of all was riding the fire-wagon. He longed to be a fireman himself and spent a lot of time at the firehouse, singing and dancing for the firemen. When the fire-alarm rang, he grabbed the coffee can and box of sandwiches that always stood near the door at the fire-house and proudly hopped on the fire-engine as it plunged wildly down the street.

Al Smith lived in a shabby street paved with cobblestones, but that street led straight to fairyland, straight to the banks of the mighty East River, where the picturesque old sailing ships

Al Smith

tied up to the wharves. As a lad, Al Smith swung from the bow-sprits of those old sailing ships and climbed in the rigging. The East River was his swimming pool, and he swam happily in his naked skin among the floating crates and driftwood.

Al Smith had what a million boys have dreamed of having—a private zoo of his own. It consisted of gaudy-colored parrots and chattering monkeys that he bought from the sailors who had brought them in from the Amazon. "When a sailor was short of funds and ready to ship again, it was easy to drive a sharp bargain with him for his monkey," Al Smith said. "For a while I had a West Indian goat, four dogs, a parrot, and a couple of monkeys—all living in peace and harmony in the garret of our house. But my mother finally made me get rid of the goat. She declared she wasn't going to have a noisy, smelly goat walking around in the garret."

The love of animals that inspired Al Smith to keep a zoo in his mother's garret also inspired him to start a zoo thirty-five years later, when he was governor of New York. This private zoo was directly behind the governor's mansion and was filled with bears, elk, deer, pheasants, foxes, alligators, and many other animals. One night someone left the monkey cage open; the monkeys escaped and a few minutes later they were traveling through the tree-tops of Albany. His Excellency Alfred Emmanuel Smith hurriedly left the affairs of state, grabbed three ripe bananas, and spent half an hour trying to coax the monkeys down from the trees. But it was no go. The monkeys took one look at the bananas the Governor held in his hand and suspected that he was up to some sort of monkey business. They did return to their cage later that night, but only because they were hungry and sleepy.

When Al Smith was fourteen years old, an event occurred that did much to mold his career. He won a speaking contest in school. This achievement gave him the limelight and developed his confidence in himself. He was soon invited to join an unusual organization, the St. James Players, a group of amateurs that put on Broadway plays in the basement of the parish churches throughout Brooklyn and New York. With their earnings they supported an orphan asylum. As an amateur actor, Al Smith was an instant success. Audiences loved his smile, his genial personality.

He soon became the star and the guiding spirit of the St. James Players. How he loved it! It whirled him away to another world. His daytime world was made up of working twelve hours a day for twelve dollars a week in the Fulton Street fish market; but at night he lived in a land of footlights and grease paint. At night he was the hero, the comedian, enjoying the spotlight, his heart swelling to sweet applause. He played the leading part in *May Blossom, The Confederate Spy, The Ticket-of-Leave Man,* and *The Almighty Dollar.* This acting experience developed in Al Smith freedom and ease before an audience, and the ability to sway a crowd. He was soon making political speeches to street-corner crowds from the back end of a truck. By this time Al was a laboring man, working with his hands in a pump factory in Brooklyn; yet as he sat eating the sandwiches that his mother had made and packed in his dinner pail for lunch, he dreamed that some day he would be elected to the New York State Assembly. This dream came true years later; but in the meantime he was given a political appointment as a process-server.

For eight years he served summonses requiring men to appear in court. This work brought him face to face with the butcher, the baker, and the financiers of Wall Street. The experience taught him a lot about human nature, and it also taught him to take abuse without flinching; for at least 20 per cent of the men on whom he served summonses denounced and cursed him.

When Al Smith arrived in Albany in January, 1904, as a new member of the State Legislature, he was thirty years old. During those thirty years he had never spent even one night in a hotel. He registered at a hotel that night, went to his room, and then read in the evening paper of a fire in a Chicago hotel in which many guests had been burned to death. It was cold that night in Albany—sixteen degrees below zero. As Al Smith sat in his room reading the gruesome details of the Chicago fire, he kept thinking of the men he had seen piling wood on the huge fire roaring in the fireplace of the hotel lobby. A wooden hotel. A windy night. Sparks might catch. He looked out of his window. He was seven stories above the street. No fire escape. The future governor of New York frankly didn't relish the prospect of being burned to death—especially the first night he ever stayed in a hotel—so he persuaded a friend to sit up with him and play pinochle until five o'clock in the morning. Then they took turns at sleeping—one sitting up for an hour while the other slept, so they wouldn't be burned to death.

During his first few years in Albany, Al Smith was bewildered by the goings-on in the State Legislature. In spite of the fact that he studied all the bills that were before the legislature, he didn't know what they were all about. They were long, complicated, obscure. As far as he was concerned, they might as well have been written in the language of the Choctaw Indians. He was given important tasks for which he had no preparation whatever. He was made a member of the Committee on Banking before he had ever even been in a bank—except to serve on some banker a summons to appear in court. He was made a member of the Committee on Forests before he had ever set foot in a forest. After serving in the Legislature for fifteen months, he was so discouraged that he wanted to quit. The only reason he didn't quit was because he was ashamed to admit defeat to his mother and friends. Finally he said to himself: "I have licked other problems and I'm going to lick this one."

From then on, he worked sixteen hours a day studying bills, the mechanics of law-making, and the operation of the legislature. He is said to have been the first person who ever refused to vote for an appropriation bill containing thousands of items without first reading and understanding every word of it. He was determined to spend the taxpayers' money as carefully as he spent his own. If a certain department wanted eight Grade-A clerks, Al Smith insisted on knowing who these clerks were to be, what they were to do, and why they were needed.

Nine years after he arrived in Albany, Al Smith was made Speaker of the State Assembly and probably knew more about the government of the State than any other living man. Ten years after he wanted to quit because of his ignorance and confusion, he astounded the New York State Constitutional Convention by his knowledge of the theory and practice of state government. Elihu Root was chairman of that convention. He described Al Smith as "brilliant," and declared that he was the brainiest member of the Convention.

Al Smith was horrified, as was all New York, by the disastrous Triangle Waist Company factory fire in 1911, in which 148 people—mostly women and girls—were burned to death, many of them leaping six stories to death on the pavement. Al Smith was so shocked by the terrible tragedy that he became a crusader for better working conditions and was instrumental in giving New York State enlightened labor laws, laws eliminating fire traps, child labor, seven-day-a-week labor, sweat shops; laws reducing industrial accidents and improving sanitary conditions. This social legislation served as a model for similar legislation in many other states and in some foreign countries.

When Tom Foley, the boss of the Fourth Ward, sent Al Smith to the New York State Legislature forty-one years ago, he said to him, "Al, never make a promise that you can't keep; and if you tell anything, always tell the truth."

And Al Smith not only told the truth, but also lived the truth and fought for the truth wherever fate placed him—"East Side, West Side, all around the town," in the governor's chair, or in national politics.

HE PAID A CARTOONIST FIFTY THOUSAND
DOLLARS A YEAR TO RIDICULE HIM

THE MAN WHO PROBABLY did as much as anyone on this earth
to save England in 1940 and give us time to prepare to save ourselves, was born in the deep, dark forests of Canada and for the
first thirty-eight years of his life was known as Max Aitken.
Today he is known as Lord Beaverbrook.

How did Lord Beaverbrook help save England in 1940? Well,
do you remember the tragic days of Dunkirk and the Battle of
Britain—days when London, Liverpool, and Coventry were
exploding and burning under the impact of German bombs—
days when the very existence of the British Empire seemed all
but doomed?

On the eve of Dunkirk, Winston Churchill realized that England's output of planes had to be doubled in a few months or
England might be lost. Now doubling a nation's output of
planes in ninety days calls for a miracle, so Churchill picked a
miracle-worker for the job. Lord Beaverbrook did jump England's plane production from nine hundred a month in May to
one thousand eight hundred a month in August, 1940—and so
probably saved England from invasion, as well as changing history for a thousand years to come.

Lord Beaverbrook got very little education. He didn't attend school long; and when he did attend, he was far more interested in fighting the other boys than in studying. He raised
so much cain that the teacher had to whip him almost every day.

At first he failed at everything he undertook—failed at selling life insurance and sewing machines, failed at running a bowling alley, failed at running a newspaper, failed to pass an examination to enter a law school.

At twenty he didn't have a dollar. At thirty, he was worth five million dollars.

How did he do it? First, he got a job as secretary to an investment banker in Halifax, Canada, and with his driving enthusiasm he began merging banks, steel companies, and power companies. In ten years he accumulated the largest fortune ever made in Canada up to that time. But he longed for still bigger achievements.

He left Canada, went to England, plunged into politics, staged a sensational political campaign, and got himself elected to Parliament. In order to gain political power, he bought a London newspaper—the *Daily Express*—that was about to fail. He lost a million dollars on it the first year. The second year was much better: he lost only a third of a million. He finally made it produce an income of a million dollars a year. He played up sensational and shocking stories, attacked the Government, and gave his subscribers gifts, free insurance policies, and hot tips on the horse races—tips that were frequently profitable.

The circulation of the *Daily Express* skyrocketed 800 per cent. It leaped from 300,000 to 2,500,000—by far the largest daily circulation of any paper in the world. Intoxicated with success, Lord Beaverbrook bought another paper, the *Evening Standard*, and founded a third, the *Sunday Express*. Beaverbrook was now helping to make and unmake British cabinets and was largely responsible for making Lloyd George Prime Minister.

But he was denied the one thing that his heart craved most. He longed to become Prime Minister of England himself. He found that he gained riches and power, but not popularity. He knew he didn't dare let his own paper praise him, yet he longed for publicity. He declared he would rather be damned than ignored. So with characteristic dash and courage, he offered a prize for the best criticism of himself written by one of his employees.

When David Low, one of England's most brilliant cartoonists, attacked Lord Beaverbrook in a competing paper, Beaverbrook said to him, "Low, I'll give you fifty thousand dollars a year if you will work for me and ridicule me in my own paper." Low accepted the offer and frequently drew cartoons depicting his boss as an insect or a devil.

Lord Beaverbrook's appointment to the Churchill Cabinet in 1943 was the fifth position he had held in the Churchill Cabinet during three and one-half years. He had been Minister of Aircraft Production, Minister of State, Minister of Supply, and Minister of Production. And now he is Lord Privy Seal, which makes him available to do special jobs for Winston Churchill.

In England Lord Beaverbrook is frequently called "The Beaver." When he was made a Peer, he chose the name Beaverbrook because, as a boy back in the woods of Canada, he had often fished in a little stream called Beaver Brook. He rides horseback almost every day and he frequently sings Negro spirituals as he gallops through the woods.

He has a private motion-picture theater on his country estate and he saw one picture—*Destry Rides Again*—twenty-seven times.

Lord Beaverbrook used to have two barbers work on him at the same time; one shaved him while the other cut his hair. Finally in order to save time, he bought an electric hair-cutter and cut his own hair.

He bought the smallest of midget radios, hung it around his neck with a cord, and danced to its music. He has telephones in every room of his great country estate, including the bathroom, and he often makes long distance calls while soaking in the tub.

He pays as high as forty dollars for a pair of shoes, and then buys a suit of clothes for about half that amount. He has his shirts made to order—expensive shirts. Yet when the buttons fall off his cuffs, he will sometimes hold them together with safety pins.

Lord Beaverbrook has a graveyard cross erected in a field near his country house. This cross is lighted at night by flood lamps. It doesn't mark a grave. But it does remind Lord Beaverbrook that *tempus fugit,* that life is fleeting, and that he should make the most of every hour because death is waiting for him out there in the tomorrows.

A REWARD OF 200,000 DOLLARS WAS OFFERED FOR HIM, DEAD OR ALIVE

On November 11, 1918, the guns on the Western Front ceased firing. Four years of bloody war, fought mostly on French soil, had come to an end. A glorious passage in Allied arms and courage had been written all the way from Belgium to the Alps with the high tide at Verdun—and the battle cry of the French Poilu, "They Shall not Pass."

Twenty years later another and greater war had come upon the world and France lay stricken and dying. In her mortal agony the voice of only one man was raised to deliver a message of burning hope and inspiration. But he was tried in a military court in 1940, found guilty, and condemned to death as a traitor. He is one of the most hated men on earth and one of the most beloved. His name is General Charles De Gaulle.

When France was crushed by the fast-spinning wheels of Germany's Panzer divisions, De Gaulle refused to surrender. He refused to recognize the outrageous terms of the armistice signed by the leaders of France. He flew to England, where he carried on the fight for France's freedom.

The German-dominated Vichy Government officially declared General De Gaulle a traitor and offered 200,000 dollars for his capture. But to the millions of Frenchmen who were living under the threat of German bayonets, General De Gaulle was the symbol of freedom.

Do you remember Armistice Day, 1918? It was the most ex-

211

citing night since the beginning of time. From the dawn of creation there never was such world-wide excitement, such hope, such rejoicing, as there was that night. After four years of bloody slaughter, after eight and one-half million men had been killed, Germany surrendered. All of us firmly believed, back in 1918, that there would be no more wars. And the second World War probably would not have occurred if France had only listened to just one man, General Charles De Gaulle.

If France had created the ten armored divisions that De Gaulle advocated, Hitler would never have dared to send his legions goose-stepping into the Rhineland. Hitler would never have dared to attack Austria and Poland.

General Charles De Gaulle was one of the first men to see clearly what modern war would be like. He was the first man to write a book describing the blitzkrieg of the future. Nine years ago General De Gaulle, in *The Army of the Future,* described the lightning war that was about to rip the world apart.

The men who were running the military affairs of France had built a wall of steel and concrete and artillery facing the German border. They called it the Maginot Line. They were preparing to fight in the future the same kind of war that they had fought from 1914 to 1918—a war of trenches, a war of huge masses of infantry moving forward slowly on foot.

But General De Gaulle warned the military leaders of France that in the next war the Maginot Line would be useless. He warned that in the next war Germany would attack France by rushing across Belgium and then pouring into France across the two hundred miles of the French-Belgian frontier where there was no Maginot Line. He pointed out that the French Army was preparing to meet this lightning-like attack with a maneuver that Napoleon had invented back in the days when muskets could be fired only twice a minute. De Gaulle warned that the wars of the future would be fought with the speed of gasoline engines, engines shooting armored cars and tanks across the country at almost a mile a minute, engines hurling airplanes through the sky at four hundred miles an hour.

But the military leaders of France pooh-poohed De Gaulle's ideas. General Petain declared De Gaulle's book was a joke, and the renowned General Weygand denounced it as an evil criticism of the French Army. Build ten motorized divisions? Absurd! Where could the factories be found to build that many tanks and armored cars? How could they be paid for? How could they be refueled on the battlefield? How could they fight in wooded hills and in mud?

No, the whole idea was ridiculous, preposterous, fantastic. That's what the French thought. But the Germans didn't. The Germans not only read De Gaulle's book. They studied it. They put it into practice. In fact, the man in charge of the Nazi mechanized army said in the presence of Hitler himself that General De Gaulle had taught the Nazis everything they knew about motorized warfare.

The Nazis were young men, hungry for new and revolutionary ideas. They built their Panzer divisions precisely as De Gaulle had advocated, and with these armored divisions, they won the swiftest and greatest victory ever recorded in all the annals of warfare. In forty-one days a hundred thousand Germans operating tanks and airplanes defeated a French army of five million. Yes, five thousand tanks and three thousand airplanes demoralized and defeated five million foot-soldiers.

In less than six weeks the mighty Republic of France was brought to her knees, and the Germans captured two million French prisoners. Two million soldiers captured—nothing like it had ever been known before in all history! To paraphrase Winston Churchill's immortal phrase: never before had so few conquered so many so quickly.

But during those six dreadful weeks, De Gaulle proved that he could fight as well as write. The Germans swept across France toward the sea, unchecked, until they met De Gaulle's mechanized force at Abbeville. There, in the only successful engagement of the war in France, De Gaulle broke through the German lines.

I once interviewed Commandant Pierre Benedictus, a French officer connected with the Fighting French Military Mission in New York. Commandant Benedictus worked with General De Gaulle in London for a year and a half, and he told me that he admired De Gaulle more than he admired any other man in the world. He told me that although De Gaulle was dignified and cold in appearance, yet inside him there was a flame that could burst out into a brilliant light.

His employees stand in awe of him, yet they admire him intensely. Even his closest associates never call him Charles. They always refer to him as "My General." He loves to read books on history, philosophy, and economics. He is deeply religious, attends church regularly, and prays every night.

General De Gaulle is a very shy man and his shyness causes him to be stiff, formal, and frigidly polite. His own mother once declared that he was so cold he must have fallen into an icebox.

Once when he was a young captain in the Army, De Gaulle met an attractive French girl in an art gallery in Paris. It took all the courage he could summon up to ask her to have tea with him that afternoon. He was so nervous that he spilled his tea on her dress. Five months later he married her.

During the first World War, General De Gaulle was wounded three times. The last time he was hit by shrapnel at Verdun, and as he lay stunned he was taken prisoner by a German patrol. He escaped five times, was recaptured five times, and spent most of the remainder of the war in solitary confinement. One of his escapes he managed by digging a tunnel with a nail file.

General De Gaulle landed in England by airplane on June 18, 1940, with no staff, no money, no troops. Winston Churchill welcomed him enthusiastically and urged him to broadcast messages of hope to the bewildered millions in defeated France. De

General Charles De Gaulle

Gaulle declared in his broadcast that day that although France had lost a battle, it hadn't lost a war; and he begged French soldiers and French workers to join him in England.

In response to his appeal, recruits began to gather from all over the world. French soldiers stole cars, rode to the Channel, and paddled to England on rafts. Some stole planes and flew to England. A student pilot who had been in the air only fifteen hours built a plane out of parts of three wrecked planes and flew to Gibraltar. Five French schoolboys paddled across the Channel in two twelve-foot canoes and landed in England, still carrying their schoolbooks.

This was merely the beginning. De Gaulle soon won over five of the French Colonies in Africa, then the French territory in India, then the French islands in the Pacific. And finally the Fighting French under General De Gaulle's leadership forced the Vichy French to surrender Syria.

De Gaulle declared that as long as France was in chains, he would fight under the cross of Lorraine and with one of the battle cries of the French Revolution—"Victory or death! Freedom or the grave!"

HE NEVER SAW A RAILROAD TRAIN UNTIL HE WAS SEVENTEEN; YET HE BECAME ONE OF THE MOST INFLUENTIAL MEN IN THE WORLD

IN THE CLOSING DAYS of the Civil War, a young man in the hills of Tennessee, whose name was Billy Hull, traded a cow to a neighbor for a gun. A few weeks later the neighbor was sorry he had parted with his musket; so he went to Billy Hull's house at night and stole the gun. Naturally, that kind of a low-down trick made Billy Hull powerful mad; so he went to his neighbor's home, called him a list of unprintable names, and forced him to return the gun. The thief swore he would get even with Billy Hull; and he did. He informed Yankee guerilla soldiers who were operating in the neighborhood that Billy Hull was stealing muskets to sell to the Confederate soldiers. The Yankee soldiers tracked Billy Hull through the hills and shot him; they thought they had killed him. A bullet passed through his head, blinding him in one eye, but in some miraculous manner it missed his brain. A farmer's wife found him and nursed him back to health. Billy Hull lived fifty-eight years longer and became a sort of legend in middle Tennessee.

Billy Hull had no formal education whatever—he could barely read and write. He became a shrewd trader, however, and was worth a fifth of a million dollars when he died in 1923. But to the end of his days, Uncle Billy Hull refused to wear a collar. He said that collars choked him and hurt his neck.

216

Cordell Hull

During the latter part of his life he used to go to Florida for the winter. He would put about five dollars' worth of clothes in a paper suitcase, tie a tin cup to the handle of the suitcase, and then travel to Florida, not in a passenger train, but in the caboose of a freight train.

But I am getting away from my story. . . . The man I really want to tell you about is not Billy Hull, but his son, Cordell Hull. When Billy Hull was a young man, he married a tall, dark Virginia girl with Cherokee Indian blood in her veins. They reared a family of five sons. Their third son was named Cordell, but they called him "Cord" for short. Cord was born in 1871, six years after the close of the Civil War. Billy Hull described his son Cordell in these words: "Cord wasn't set enough to be a schoolteacher, wasn't rough enough to be a lumberman, wasn't sociable enough to be a doctor, and couldn't holler loud enough to be a preacher. But Cord was a right thorough thinker." X

Not only was Cordell Hull a right thorough thinker, but he also became a right thorough statesman. For the last eleven years he has been our Secretary of State. The son of Billy Hull and the girl with Cherokee blood in her veins now stands in the front ranks of the statesmen who are running the world.

The story of Cordell Hull's life is largely a story of law and politics. He served in Congress for twenty-two years and has spent more than two-thirds of his life in public office. He declares that he can't even remember the time when he wasn't determined to become a lawyer. He was so determined to become a lawyer that he wouldn't go fishing or swimming with the other boys. He sat on a tree stump reading books while they fished for mud-cats and dived in the old swimming hole. His father said, "Cord was always just like a growed-up man from the time he could walk."

As a boy, Cordell Hull used to help his father float rafts of timber down to Nashville. The trip down the river took ten days and nights, during which time Cordell slept under the open sky, rain or shine. He loved—well, I was about to say he loved the work of rafting. But the truth is that in spite of the hard labor, he didn't regard rafting logs down the river as work at all. Instead, it was his favorite sport, a thrilling adventure into the new world of Nashville, with its trains and hotels and fine carriages. For him, the chief attraction of Nashville was its bookstores, where he spent the little money he had for second-hand law books.

In his long public career, extending over half a century, Cordell Hull has made many speeches; but he himself declares he made the most important speech of his life when he was fourteen years old. It was like this: Cordell knew that his father was going to send one of his five sons to college, but which one he hadn't quite decided. Cordell was determined that he was going to be the one selected for higher education. In order to impress his father, Cordell joined the debating society at the Willow Grove school. In one debate Cordell was supposed to prove that George Washington deserved more credit for defending America than Columbus deserved for discovering it. Cordell knew that his father would be present to hear him debate this burning question, and so would all the neighbors for miles around. He worked day and night, studying histories, collecting facts, rehearsing his speech. The County Teachers Association was holding a convention that week in Willow Grove and Cordell even buttonholed every teacher attending that convention and asked him which he felt deserved more credit, Washington or Columbus, and why. Cordell won the debate and, sure enough, his father sent him twelve miles away from home to attend a little school called the Montvale Academy.

While attending the academy, Cordell Hull rented a room in town, cooked his own meals, washed his dishes, and made his bed. On Friday nights he would walk twelve miles home to his father's farm, arriving in time to take part in the program of the Willow Grove Debating Society. On Monday morning he would leave the farm and walk twelve miles back to town, carrying with him some hoecake his mother had baked, and home-cured bacon. Living in town under these conditions cost Cordell Hull about thirty cents a day.

Montvale Academy could hardly be called the Harvard of the South. It had only two teachers, but one of these pedagogues, Joe McMillin, not only taught Cordell Hull surveying, anatomy, geometry, and Greek; but he also did something a thousand times more important—he sharpened the boy's vision and ambition, and inspired him with an abiding confidence in his own powers.

A large framed motto that hung on the walls of the Montvale Academy was probably responsible, to some degree, for Cordell Hull's lifelong habit of working twelve to fourteen hours a day. The motto read: "There is no excellence without great labor."

Cordell Hull had only one ambition in those days: he wanted to be a politician. He knew that in order to be a successful politician he had to make speeches, so he studied public speaking and recited poems before the school on Friday afternoons. His favorite poem was "Bingen on the Rhine."

Cordell's desire to speak well was so intense that he took thirty dollars his father had paid him for doing chores on the farm, hired a horse and buggy, and drove a congressman, Benton McMillin, from town to town, so that he could study this political speaker's talks day by day. This congressman afterward became governor of Tennessee. Cordell Hull admits that his political career was deeply influenced by listening to and absorbing McMillin's speeches on foreign trade and tariffs.

Cordell Hull got his law degree at Cumberland University Law School, and started practicing law before he was old enough to vote. His clients were as scarce as rainbows, so he spent most of his time reading Blackstone's *Commentaries* and playing poker with the older lawyers, listening to their experiences and advice.

Even at that early date Cordell Hull was already interested in

219

world affairs; he was one of the few men in town who subscribed to a weekly paper printed in Nashville. That paper, *The Weekly American,* arrived by steamboat two or three days after publication. News of the outside world was so scarce in that part of Tennessee that people gathered in absorbed circles around Cordell Hull while he read the news aloud.

Plunging into politics, he got himself elected to the state legislature before he was old enough to be admitted to that body; but the legislature didn't meet until after his twenty-first birthday, so that problem solved itself.

At thirty-two he was made a circuit court judge and spent eleven months out of the year riding the circuit with horse and buggy, just as Abe Lincoln had done half a century earlier. The people down in Tennessee still refer to him as Judge Hull, and so does his wife when she is talking to strangers.

As a judge, Cordell Hull was strict and impartial. He once fined his own father five dollars for sitting in court with his hat on. On another occasion he refused to listen to the plea of the woman who had nursed his father back to health after he had been shot by Yankee soldiers and left for dead. This woman came to Judge Hull, pleading for her son, who had been arrested for disturbing church services. "If the jury convicts my boy and you fine him," she said, "he'll have to go to jail and I'll have to go to the poorhouse." The jury found the boy guilty, and Judge Hull fined him fifty dollars. Then he reached down into his own pocket and gave the boy's mother a hundred dollars in cash, fifty for the fine and fifty for herself—more cash than a mountain family was likely to make in two or three years.

At the age of thirty-five, Cordell Hull battled his way through an exciting campaign for Congress and won by only seventeen votes, after driving all over the rough roads of his district and breaking three buggy wheels and two sets of buggy springs.

When he arrived in Washington in 1906, he realized that if he wanted to get ahead in politics, he would have to become a specialist in something. As a result, he has been studying, talking, and living taxes and tariffs for a third of a century. Thirty-one years ago he wrote the first income-tax laws that this nation ever had; twenty-eight years ago he wrote our first inheritance-tax laws. His interest in tariff is almost fanatical. He says he prefers a "seven-page pamphlet on tariff figures to a seven-course dinner."

That is probably correct, for he despises long dinners and never accepts social invitations except to official dinners that he can't possibly dodge. Even then, he doesn't eat the dinners; instead, he eats some chicken and some salad and drinks a glass of milk before he leaves home.

Hull didn't marry until he was forty-six years old. Then he married a charming Virginia widow. They have no children. They live in a seven-room apartment at the Hotel Carlton in Washington. Hull frequently answers the door himself.

A lot of people, including the Japs, have found it difficult to slip anything over on Cordell Hull. A month before Pearl Harbor, he kept warning us: "Japan will strike soon. Japan will strike soon." But even the people at Pearl Harbor paid no attention.

Such is the story of Cordell Hull, the barefoot boy from the backwoods of Tennessee, who never saw a railroad train until he was seventeen years old.

HE STARTED IN A PHOTOGRAPHER'S SHOP AND BECAME THE WORLD'S GREATEST BUILDER OF SHIPS

THE BUSINESS MAN whom the war brought most rapidly to the fore, is Henry J. Kaiser. He probably did as much as any other civilian on earth to win the war. Few people had ever heard of Henry J. Kaiser before the war; but in a few short years—well, his gigantic activities were truly astonishing. He had seven huge shipbuilding yards going full blast night and day, turning out freight ships, tankers, frigates, destroyers, troop transports, and aircraft carriers.

Kaiser also was operating a fighter-plane factory and a plane-parts factory.

He built and operated a big, new magnesium plant, turning out vast quantities of the new lightweight miracle metal that is so vital in modern war.

When he was unable to get the steel he needed, Kaiser built the first integrated steel mill ever erected west of the Rocky Mountains—everything from blast furnaces to rolling mills. He then bought an iron mine to supply ore for his steel mill and he bought coal mines to get fuel for his furnaces.

Through his other companies, Kaiser and his partners helped raise the battleships sunk at Pearl Harbor. They helped build several naval air bases on Wake Island, Midway, and Guam. They built a part of the military highway to Alaska; built military airports and radio stations in Alaska, drilled for oil, erected

222

Henry J. Kaiser

an oil refinery, and laid a four-hundred-mile pipe line in the far north; and they installed a set of locks on the Panama Canal.

Kaiser owns the world's largest cement plant. He played a major role in building three of the world's largest dams: Boulder Dam, on the Colorado River; the Bonneville Dam, on the Columbia River in Oregon (a job that many engineers declared to be impossible); and Grand Coulee, also on the Columbia River—the biggest dam on earth.

Henry Kaiser became one of the largest employers of labor in America.

Plain folks everywhere feel that this man Kaiser—big, fat, baldheaded—is one of them. He belongs. They like him because he is plain and folksy and enthusiastic.

Before the war, Kaiser had never built even a flat-bottom rowboat. Within four years he became the biggest and fastest builder of ships the world had ever known.

He revolutionized one of the oldest businesses known to man, the business of building ships. For example, shipbuilders used to figure on taking six months to build a ship. But Kaiser's Oregon shipbuilding corporation built a Liberty Ship in ten days. When the men in Kaiser's California shipbuilding yard heard about that record, they swore that they would outdo the Oregon boys at that game. They pitched in and—well, to be specific, they laid the keel of a ship called *The Robert E. Peary* at one minute past midnight on Sunday morning and slid her into the water, 90 per cent complete, on the following Thursday afternoon. Think of doing in four and a half days a job that used to take six months, sometimes a whole year!

Of course, it was a stunt performance. It couldn't possibly be kept up every week; but Kaiser continued to turn out Liberty Ships from keel to delivery in less than a month.

Kaiser loves to work under pressure, loves to roar through life with a head of steam up, loves to tackle jobs that the experts say can't be done. When he proposed to build ships on an

223

assembly line, he knew nothing whatever about building ships. He had seen a shipyard but once in his life before he started building one of his own. But he figured that maybe that was an asset—maybe it was a good thing not to know what couldn't be done. He refused to build ships in the old way, by laying a keel and then building the ship up from that. That method was too slow for war. Kaiser ordered his engineers to build a shipyard three times as big as the ordinary shipyard, a yard so big that thousands of men could work in it at one time, so that the bow section of the ship could be built in one place, the stern in another, the galley in another.

When all these parts were finished, a huge crane, far bigger than had ever been used in a shipyard before, picked them up and lowered them in place on the ship. These pieces were largely welded in place. Kaiser used a minimum of rivets—rivets were too slow for him.

Another Kaiser novelty was to assemble parts of ships in assembly lines, just as automobiles are manufactured. Still another new idea of Kaiser and his engineers was to build a lot of sections—deckhouses, for instance—upside down. That permitted workmen to use downhand welding, which is easier and faster than overhead welding. When the parts were finished, a crane turned them rightside up, picked them up, and dropped them in place.

Even as a boy, Henry J. Kaiser displayed the vision, the enthusiasm, the restless, driving ambition that were destined to make him rich and famous. His German-born father, a shoemaker, could hardly make enough money to support his family of four children. Since Henry was the only boy in the family, he had to quit school when he was eleven years of age and go to work. He got a job in Utica, New York, delivering parcels for a department store by day. But he devoted his nights to the passion of his youth, photography. Devouring all the books on photography he could find at the public library, he later got a job working for a photographer in the near-by resort town of Lake Placid, New York. But to Henry J. Kaiser this new job wasn't work. It was fun, play, joy. He devoted all of his waking hours to it, injecting a new life, a new enthusiasm into the business of selling photographic supplies and developing and printing pictures for amateurs. He even made picture postcards of Lake Placid scenes—postcards that sold like buckwheat cakes and honey. Within one year Henry Kaiser owned a half-interest in the business. Within three years he owned the business outright. Within five years, he had opened photographic shops in Palm Beach and Daytona Beach, Florida. Yet today Kaiser doesn't even own a camera.

Yearning for larger worlds to conquer, Kaiser left his photographic business and rushed out to the Pacific Northwest, where a new empire was being built. He got a job as salesman for the Hawkeye Sand & Gravel Company of Spokane, and bought stock in the company, paying for it out of his weekly earnings.

One day he called on a Chicago construction company that had landed a big construction job for the city of Spokane. He called to sell his line of supplies. He didn't sell any supplies, but he did sell himself. The Chicago company hired him on the spot.

When Kaiser was twenty-nine years old, he gave up his salaried position and went in business for himself. His only possessions were some second-hand wheelbarrows and concrete-mixers, and four horses, all of which he had bought on credit. But he had other assets—not so easy to see, but much more important—tremendous assets of energy, experience, judgment, enthusiasm, and undying determination to get ahead. Within two months he landed a job of street paving—a job amounting to a quarter of a million dollars. He was heading for the big money now. Within a few years his firm paved a thousand miles of highways on the Pacific Coast.

Henry Kaiser has said repeatedly that he isn't interested in money. That's right. He isn't. He will never have time to spend even a fraction of what he has. He has no time for hobbies, little time for reading, picture shows, or vacations—little time for anything but work. The more work he can pack into twenty-four hours, the happier he is. He has a suite of rooms in a hotel in Washington, D. C., another suite in the Waldorf-Astoria in New York. He spends several hours a day holding conferences on the long-distance telephone. He has all his key-executives from the Atlantic to the Pacific cut into the same telephone circuit, so they can all listen and take part in a discussion of Kaiser's problems. The cost? Oh, in one year he sometimes spends on telephone calls about a fifth of a million dollars. He swamps Government officials with telegrams two feet long, pleading, threatening, demanding this or that. He rarely sleeps more than five hours a night. How the man lives in such a whirlwind of work and excitement without dropping dead from heart failure or apoplexy is a mystery.

Kaiser built his summer home at Lake Tahoe, Nevada, 6500 feet up in the Sierra Nevada mountains. The way he built that house is characteristic of the way he does everything. Rushing bulldozers and steam shovels and cranes to Lake Tahoe, he quickly tore out the forest, ripped up the earth, and filled up marshes. He did all this with crews working day and night under glaring floodlights. He built a large stone house, four guest cottages, and a boathouse in twenty-eight days, rushing them through with a feverish speed, as if the future of civilization were hanging in the balance. That's Kaiser for you!

Throughout the war, the Government was his one giant customer. Will Henry Kaiser be able to carry on his mighty war-born empire in the face of competition and vastly altered conditions? Many people believe he won't, but he hopes he will. He has created a Development and Engineering Division, a division run by engineers, scientists, inventors, research men, and business specialists—men with the ability to think on a

226

large scale and the imagination to create new products and new industries to keep employment high during the post-war period.

He believes that with new and lighter materials he can build fast passenger ships that can operate so economically that countless thousands who never traveled before will be able to afford ocean voyages.

As for automobiles: "I'm disgusted," Henry Kaiser says, "when I see a 3000-pound car carrying a 150-pound man." He threatens to build of lightweight metals, plywood, and plastics, cars that will weigh only one-third as much as our present autos and will be powered by engines burning the one hundred percent octane fuel we now use in our airplanes.

He also hopes to go in for quantity production of a plane so safe that Grandma can fly it and so cheap that Grandpa can buy it.

Yes, Henry J. Kaiser is a roaring optimist. "You can't sit on the lid of progress. If you do," he says, "you will be blown to pieces."

THEY MADE HISTORY IN TWELVE SECONDS

Do you have a boy? If so, do you realize that some toy or some book that you give him may change his life? To illustrate: In 1878, a Bishop of the United Brethren Church was living in Cedar Rapids, Iowa. One day while traveling on church business, he bought a mechanical toy for his two young sons. As he returned home one June day, his two sons ran to greet him and he said, "Boys, I've got something for you—catch." And he tossed an object toward them. But this object, instead of traveling in their direction, did an incredible thing. It actually flew up to the ceiling, fluttered there a few seconds, and then fell to the floor. The boys screamed and ran to pick it up, pop-eyed with excitement.

It was a toy flying machine about six inches long, made out of cork, bamboo, and paper. It was kept aloft by two propellers that whirled in opposite directions. These tiny paper propellers were run by twisted rubber bands. That toy developed in these boys an interest in flying that finally inspired them to invent a flying machine that has affected everybody reading this story. No other invention since the invention of gunpowder thousands of years ago has so changed man's method of waging war.

Those boys were named Wright—Wilbur and Orville Wright.

The Wright brothers played with this toy flying machine that their father brought home until it was broken to pieces.

The Wright Brothers

Since they had no money to buy another one, they built one themselves. Later they began building and flying kites that were so superb that the other boys in town bought them.

From that time on, Wilbur and Orville Wright were obsessed with a desire to fly. They would lie on their backs for hours watching their kites fluttering in the air, watching the flight of swallows and sparrows and pigeons, watching hawks soaring on wind currents for half an hour without flapping a wing.

One day they were deeply impressed by a dispatch in a Dayton, Ohio, paper telling of an engineer in Berlin, Germany, by the name of Otto Lilenthal, who had met his death while trying to fly. This man Lilenthal had been gliding off and on for years on a pair of huge wings strapped tò his shoulders and a tail strapped to his body. He could glide downhill only, but even that was nearer to flying than man had ever come before.

Reading that article was a turning point in the lives of Wilbur and Orville Wright. Why? Because Lilenthal had demonstrated that it really was possible for a man to glide on the winds like the hawks in the air.

Wilbur and Orville Wright had gotten hold of an idea that soon became a passion, an obsession. They wrote the Smithsonian Institution in Washington and got a list of all the scientific articles that had ever been written on human flight. They read and studied these articles with enthusiasm.

Finally, after four years of study, they decided to build a glider themselves, just for fun. They didn't dream of inventing a machine that would revolutionize our conception of time and space and transform the geography of the world. But that is precisely what their invention did do, for the speed of the airplane has brought every spot on earth to within sixty hours of your home. It has made the earth about one-fifth as large as it used to be—in many ways, one-tenth as large as it used to be.

Did Orville and Wilbur Wright consider themselves scientists or inventors? Oh, no, nothing of the kind. Just a couple of young men having some sport at flying, in their spare time, just as other men get sport out of skiing or mountain climbing.

Since they had to make a living, they ran a small shop in Dayton, Ohio, where they sold and repaired bicycles. The only time they had left in which to experiment with their dream was at night after the shop was closed.

They built their first glider for a total cost of fifteen dollars. It had two wings, one on top of the other, no body and no tail; but it did have a little contraption out in front to steer it. It had no engine, of course.

The Wright boys decided to spend their vacation time trying to fly in this glider. They learned from the United States Weather Bureau that conditions were just right at Kill Devil Hill, Kitty Hawk, North Carolina. There a strong wind is always sweeping in from the sea and the ground is always soft with billowy sand. They tried their glider at Kitty Hawk, and it worked after a fashion. It did carry them, one at a time downhill on the wind, but it would stay in the air for only a few seconds. The next year they built a larger and better glider. Again the results were discouraging—so discouraging that Wilbur Wright declared that man wouldn't learn to fly for a thousand years. They were ready to give up all attempts at flying and probably would never have invented the airplane at all if a distinguished engineer had not encouraged them. The dynamite he used was honest appreciation and encouragement. His name was Octave Chanute, and he had written a book entitled *Progress in Flying Machines*. This book made him an authority on flying. After watching the Wright brothers glide at Kitty Hawk, he told them that in spite of their poor results and discouragement, they had broken all records for distance and that they were now the two most successful flyers the world had ever known.

They were astonished, cheered, and bucked up to hear those words of praise from a distinguished man like Octave Chanute.

The Wright Brothers

Astonished because they had never gone to college, had had no technical training whatever. They were again astonished and pleased when Octave Chanute invited Wilbur to make a speech about his experiments on flying before the Western Society of Engineers in Chicago.

Wilbur Wright proposed to say in his Chicago speech that all the tables prepared by the scientists, setting forth the effect of wind on airplane wings, were absolutely wrong. But his brother Orville was alarmed by such a sweeping criticism; and, as a precaution, Orville decided to test the figures. He took an empty wooden starch box about eighteen inches long, knocked out both ends, and put a mechanical fan at one end to create a wind. He put a glass top in the box so he could look in and see what effect the wind was having on different sizes and shapes of tiny airplane wings. Little did he dream at the time that he was building the world's first wind tunnel, and little did he dream that he, a mere self-taught bicycle repair man, was proving that all the wind pressure tables compiled by the learned scientists were absolutely wrong. Without the knowledge Orville Wright obtained by these wind tunnel tests, neither the Wright brothers nor anyone else could possibly have built an airplane that would fly.

These tests uncovered the technical facts on which modern aviation is founded—and the Wright brothers would probably never have made these tests had it not been for the speech Wilbur had to give in Chicago.

The Wright brothers made over a thousand successful flights with the last glider they built; but they were exasperated because they could rarely find suitable winds for gliding. Usually the winds were too light, or too strong, or too gusty and jerky. In desperation, they made a decision that revolutionized the history of man's attempt to fly. That decision was this: they decided to make their own wind. How? By putting a gasoline engine in their plane and connecting it with propellers. Since

231

no manufacturer made the kind of lightweight motor they desired, they built one themselves, in their bicycle shop at night. They built the entire machine, motor and all, for less than eight hundred dollars.

With this machine, on December 17, 1903, they made the first flight in the annals of history, from Kill Devil Hill at Kitty Hawk, North Carolina. It was a biting cold day and the men, tinkering with the plane, slapped their arms to keep warm. But cold as it was, Orville Wright wouldn't wear an overcoat when he mounted the plane, because an overcoat would mean additional weight.

At exactly thirty-five minutes past ten o'clock, Orville Wright climbed on the roaring craft, stretched out flat on his stomach, and pulled the release. The strange machine belched flames from the open exhaust and then rose into the air, snorting and leaping like a bucking broncho. The impossible had happened —a heavier-than-air machine had actually soared into the air and flown for 120 feet! That was one of the most important and significant events in human history. Yet Orville Wright admitted that he didn't get any thrill out of this historic achievement. He said he expected the darn thing to work, and it did. That was all.

When the Wright brothers returned home after making the first successful flight in all history, what happened? Were they met by a reception committee and a brass band? No, nobody met them. True, one of their home town newspapers mentioned the flight, but only casually, as if it were of no importance.

A year later the Wright brothers were making almost daily flights of twenty-five miles—long flights over a cow pasture near Dayton, Ohio. But the Dayton newspapers didn't even mention these miracles. The papers went right on publishing the fact that Cy Jones was recovering from a severe cold, that Mrs. Smith had returned home after visiting her mother; but about the flying machine in the cow pasture—the flying machine that was destined to transform geography and revolutionize the art of waging war—not one word.

For a long time the scientific magazines also refused to publish a word about the Wright brothers' flying machine. Why? Because they thought it either wasn't true or wasn't important. The first magazine that did publish an article about it was, of all things, a magazine devoted to the business of producing honey, a magazine called *Gleanings in Bee Culture*.

For three years the Wright brothers tried repeatedly to persuade the War Department to send a man to Dayton, Ohio, to see their flying machine in action. They felt it might be valuable for scouting purposes in war time. But these hard-boiled Army officers in Washington just couldn't believe that anything so fantastic as a flying machine could be practical.

Finally, almost four years after the first flight had been made, the War Department decided to purchase one plane; so it advertised for bids. Imagine advertising for bids when there was only one concern in the world that could possibly make a plane that would fly! Sounds like Gilbert and Sullivan.

Wilbur Wright died of typhoid fever in 1912, but Orville Wright is living today in Dayton, Ohio, at 72. He has never married, is extremely modest, doesn't care for titles, honors or money, dislikes publicity, and refuses to talk to newspaper reporters.

That first flight made by Orville and Wilbur Wright lasted only twelve seconds, but these twelve seconds thundered in a new and mighty epoch in human history, for at long last the great dream of the ages had come true. At long last, man had shaken off the shackles of earth and soared up toward the stars.